BEOWULF

Seamus Heaney, translator

Teacher Guide

Written by
Pat Watson

Edited by
Heather M. Johnson

Note

The new verse translation paperback, published by W.W. Norton & Company, © 2000 by Seamus Heaney, was used to prepare this guide. The page references may differ in other editions.

Please note: This novel unit deals with sensitive, mature issues. Parts may contain descriptions of violence. Please assess the appropriateness of this book for the age level and maturity of your students prior to reading and discussing it with them.

ISBN 1-58130-800-0

Copyright infringement is a violation of Federal Law.

© 2003, 2004 by Novel Units, Inc., Bulverde, Texas. All rights reserved. No part of this publication may be reproduced, translated, stored in a retrieval system, or transmitted in any way or by any means (electronic, mechanical, photocopying, recording, or otherwise) without prior written permission from Novel Units, Inc.

Photocopying of student worksheets by a classroom teacher at a non-profit school who has purchased this publication for his/her own class is permissible. Reproduction of any part of this publication for an entire school or for a school system, by for-profit institutions and tutoring centers, or for commercial sale is strictly prohibited.

Novel Units is a registered trademark of Novel Units, Inc.

Printed in the United States of America.

To order, contact your local school supply store, or—

Novel Units, Inc.
P.O. Box 433
Bulverde, TX 78163-0433

Web site: www.educyberstor.com

Table of Contents

Skills and Strategies

Comprehension
Predicting, sequencing, story mapping, cause/effect, inference, summarization

Writing
Research, essay, poetry, riddle, dirge, precis

Literary Elements
Characterization, simile, metaphor, kenning, theme, symbolism, irony

Thinking
Research, compare/contrast, analysis

Vocabulary
Target words, definitions, applications

Listening/Speaking
Discussion, oral presentation

Across the Curriculum
Music—appropriate selections, ballad; Art—collage, sketch; Drama—script

Genre: epic poem

Setting (place and time): Scandinavia; land of the Geats (now southern Sweden) and Denmark; composed orally by a scop or bard sometime between the middle of the seventh and the end of the tenth century A.D., with references to earlier historical events

Point of View: third-person omniscient

Themes: courage, loyalty, perseverance, vengeance, good vs. evil

Conflict: Beowulf's three battles with his antagonists: Grendel, Grendel's mother, and the dragon

Style: noble, majestic verse, with a caesura in each line; it is organized into three main parts, each revealing one of Beowulf's conflicts

Tone: fervent when relating Beowulf's exploits; ominous when foreshadowing and revealing Beowulf's fate

Summary

Grendel, a seemingly invincible demon monster, is terrorizing King Hrothgar of Denmark and his people, relentlessly attacking and killing each night. Beowulf, a young Geat hero, comes to the aid of the Danes. He fights with and kills both Grendel and Grendel's mother, and King Hrothgar rewards him lavishly. Beowulf returns to Geatland, where he eventually becomes the king. When a dragon threatens his people, the aged Beowulf faces his final battle. With the aid of the warrior Wiglaf, Beowulf kills the dragon but is mortally wounded by the venom from the dragon's bite. His grieving people follow Beowulf's wishes and burn his body on a funeral pyre, then erect "Beowulf's Barrow" to memorialize him.

Major and Minor Characters

Beowulf: the Geat protagonist who faces and conquers evil; classic hero who is courageous, generous, and compassionate

Grendel: a demon; first antagonist Beowulf faces; descendant of Cain, outcast who epitomizes bitterness and evil; dies after Beowulf rips off his arm

Grendel's mother: unnamed demon who lives in the bog; second antagonist; dies in an attempt to avenge her son's death

The Dragon: becomes enraged and seeks vengeance when a thief takes something from his treasured hoard; third antagonist; dies after inflicting a fatal wound on Beowulf

Shield Sheafson: founder of the ruling house of the Danes

Beow: Shield's son

Halfdane: Beow's son; father of Hrothgar, Heorogar, Halga, and an unnamed daughter who marries the Swedish King Onela

Hrothgar: king of the Danes whom Beowulf goes to assist; kind, benevolent; rewards Beowulf with lavish gifts and accolades

Wealhtheow: Hrothgar's wife

Hrethric and Hrothmund: sons of Hrothgar and Wealhtheow; Hrethric is denied access to his father's throne by Hrothgar's nephew, Hrothulf

Wulfgar: first to greet the Geats; takes Beowulf's message to Hrothgar

All rights reserved

Unferth: Hrothgar's warrior who is jealous of Beowulf and challenges him verbally

Aeschere: Hrothgar's most trusted friend and advisor; killed by Grendel's mother

Ecgtheow: Beowulf's father

King Hrethel: Beowulf's foster father

Hygelac: king of the Geats

Hygd: Hygelac's wife

Breca: Beowulf's friend who challenges him to a swimming match

Wiglaf: loyal warrior who assists Beowulf in slaying the dragon

Sigemund: dragon-slayer whose legend foreshadows Beowulf's conflict with the dragon

King Heremod: legendary evil king who serves as a foil for Beowulf

Hildeburh: a Danish princess who marries the Frisian King Finn and ultimately loses her son, her brother, and her husband in bloody conflicts with the Danes

Queen Modthryth: legendary wicked queen whose cruelty contrasts with Queen Hygd's honor

Manuscript and Translator Information

Beowulf originated in England as an oral narrative in Old English, also called the Anglo-Saxon language. The poem exists only in one manuscript, presumably written around A.D. 1000, and this copy is now preserved in the British Library. It has been transcribed and translated numerous times (pp. *ix-x*). The poem is related with a Christian perspective, i.e., the events transpire in a primarily pagan culture, but the providential help of the Christian God enables Beowulf to overcome evil with good. Literary devices such as *metaphors*, *kennings*, and *alliteration* contribute to the imagery of the poem. Light and dark symbolize good and evil, e.g., the light of Hrothgar's Hall (Heorot) and Hygelac's hall in Geatland contrasts with the darkness of the habitations of Grendel, his mother, and the dragon.

Seamus Heaney, an Irish poet and resident of Dublin, teaches part-time at Harvard. He began working on this translation of *Beowulf* in the mid-1980s at the request of the editors of *The Norton Anthology of English Literature*. Heaney received the Nobel Prize in Literature in 1995. His most recent collection of poems, *Opened Ground: Selected Poems 1966–1996* (1998) features selections from ten of his poetry books.

Teaching Strategies

1. The poem is more effective if read aloud. Possibilities include (a) selecting students to read, assigning the parts at least a day in advance (b) teacher reading all or portions (c) reading silently while listening to an audio cassette: available at BookSense.com (read by Seamus Heaney).
2. Play an audio cassette of selected passages in Old English: available at Spoken Arts; 310 North Avenue; New Rochelle, N.Y. 10801; (914) 636-5482.

   See also **www.humanities.mcmaster.ca/~beowulf/main.html.** (Note: This Web site was active at the printing of this guide.)
3. The poem includes both pagan and Christian references. Students may consider an allegorical focus when responding to discussion questions and participating in activities.
4. Instances in this guide where a reference is made to "Christianity" or "Christian" refer to the monotheistic pre-Christian characters in the poem.

All rights reserved

Background Information

The following information will help students understand the poem.

1. **Anglo-Saxons:** members of Germanic tribes (Angles, Saxons, Jutes) that settled in what is now England in A.D. 400–500. These tribes quickly occupied most of southern and eastern Britain, and wars often erupted between the tribes. Seven kingdoms evolved by the 700s, and by the late 800s, Danish Vikings had attacked all the kingdoms. Only the kingdom of Wessex survived, led by Alfred the Great. Alfred's descendants eventually defeated the Vikings and assimilated Wessex and Viking territory into a kingdom they called England, meaning "Angle folk" or "land of the Angles." In 597, St. Augustine of Canterbury began converting Anglo-Saxons to Christianity.
2. **Old English:** heavily Germanic language used by the Anglo-Saxons from about A.D. 500 to 1100; foundation of today's English language
3. **Geats:** members of an ancient Germanic people of Scandinavia who were conquered by the Swedes in the A.D. 500s; Beowulf is a prince of the Geats
4. **Danes:** people from Denmark; those of Danish descent; King Hrothgar is the Danish king
5. **Swedes:** people born or living in Sweden
6. **Jutes:** members of Germanic tribes from Denmark and northern Germany; conquered most of England in A.D. 450–500; originally from an area of Denmark now known as Jutland
7. **Frisians:** people from Friesland, a northern province of the Netherlands
8. **Scandinavians:** people who live in Denmark, Norway, and Sweden
9. **Mead-hall:** gathering place for warriors; where they told stories, drank, ate, and received rewards from their king or other leader

Prereading Glossary

1. **alliteration:** repetition of identical initial consonant sounds or successive vowel sounds, e.g. the names of Halfdane's children: "Heorogar, Hrothgar, the good Halga" (p. 7) and "...Shield Sheafson, scourge of many tribes" (p. 3)
2. **allusion:** reference to a historical or literary figure, event, or object, e.g., Cain and Abel (Bible, Genesis 4)
3. **caesura:** a pause or break in the meter or rhythm of a line of verse
4. **Christian:** a person who believes in Jesus as Christ and lives according to His teachings
5. **epic:** a long narrative poem that relates the exploits of a great hero; the characters are of noble birth or are supernatural beings from the past
6. **foil:** a person who, through strong contrast, emphasizes or enhances the distinctive characteristics of another
7. **hero:** protagonist, i.e., central character in a story; enlists reader's sympathy
8. **heroic code:** the hero's moral rules of right and wrong
9. **kenning:** figurative, usually a metaphorical compound expression used in the place of a name or noun, especially in Old English, e.g., "sail-road" for ocean (p. 99) and "bone-cage" for body (p. 101)
10. **metaphor:** a comparison between two things; does not use "like" or "as"

All rights reserved

11. **pagan:** a person who worships many gods or no god
12. **simile:** a comparison between two things using "like" or "as"
13. **symbolism:** use of symbols; use of an object to represent or suggest another; i.e., something which is itself, yet suggests something else

Initiating Activities

Use one or more of the following to introduce the novel.

1. Present background information and summarize the Introduction.
2. Preview the book with students. Have them note the translator, then identify the genre, place and date of composition, length, setting, protagonist, and antagonist.
3. Play selected passages of an audio cassette in Old English.
4. Place the Vocabulary Word Map on an overhead transparency and brainstorm with students as they complete the chart.
5. Present the Prereading Glosssary and use the Vocabulary Word Map for some of the words.
6. Copy, enlarge, and display the Family Trees at the back of the book, before the Acknowledgements. Have students form groups to develop strategies to learn the relationships in the diagrams.

Vocabulary Word Map

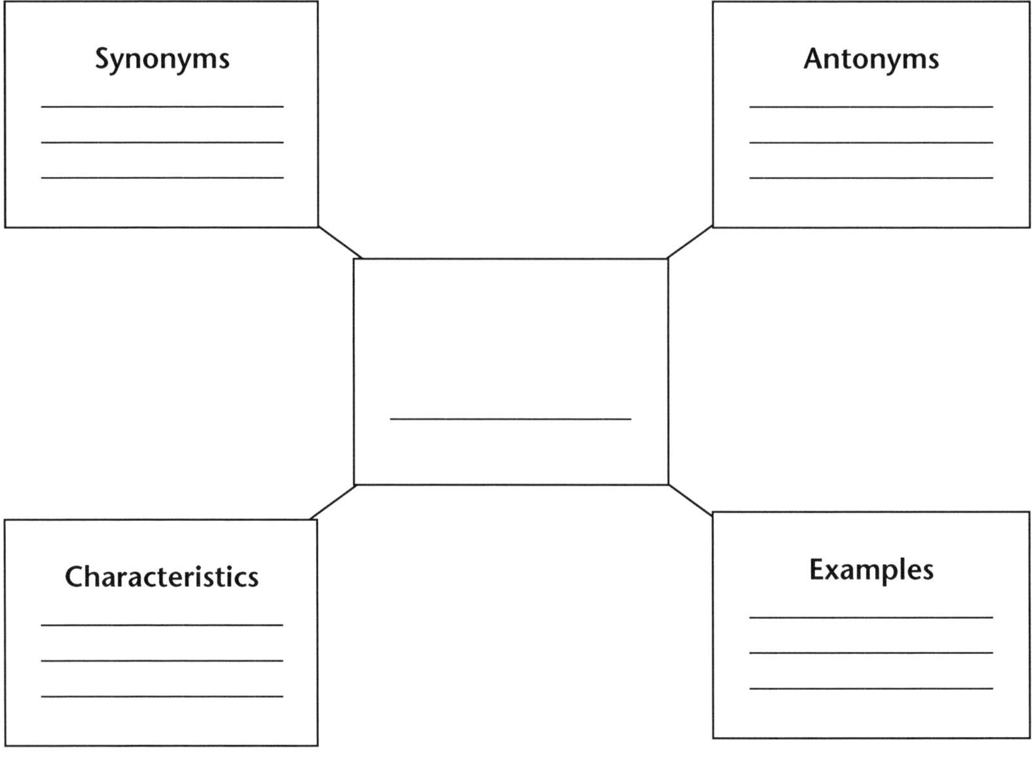

All rights reserved

© Novel Units, Inc.

Foreshadowing Chart

Foreshadowing is the literary technique of giving clues to coming events in a story.

Directions: Think about *Beowulf.* What examples of foreshadowing do you recall from the story? If necessary, skim through the chapters to find examples of foreshadowing. List at least four examples below. Explain what clues are given, then list the coming event that is suggested.

Foreshadowing	Page #	Clues	Coming Event

All rights reserved

Attribute Web

Directions: Complete the attribute web by filling in information specific to a character in the book.

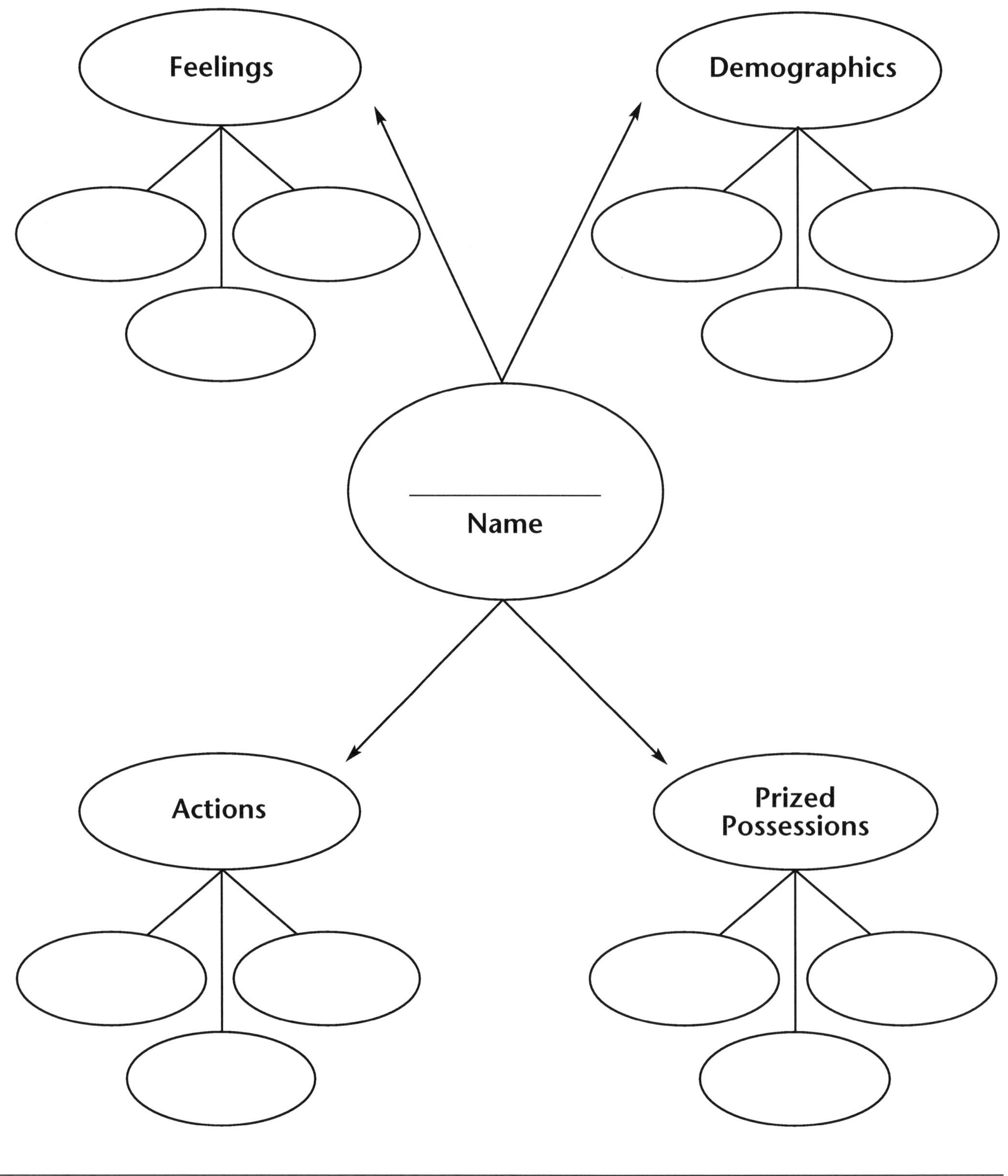

All rights reserved

© Novel Units, Inc.

Sociogram

Directions: Write the name of a different character in each circle. On the "spokes" surrounding each character's name, write several adjectives that describe that character. On the arrows joining one character to another, write a description of the relationship between the two characters. How does one character influence the other?

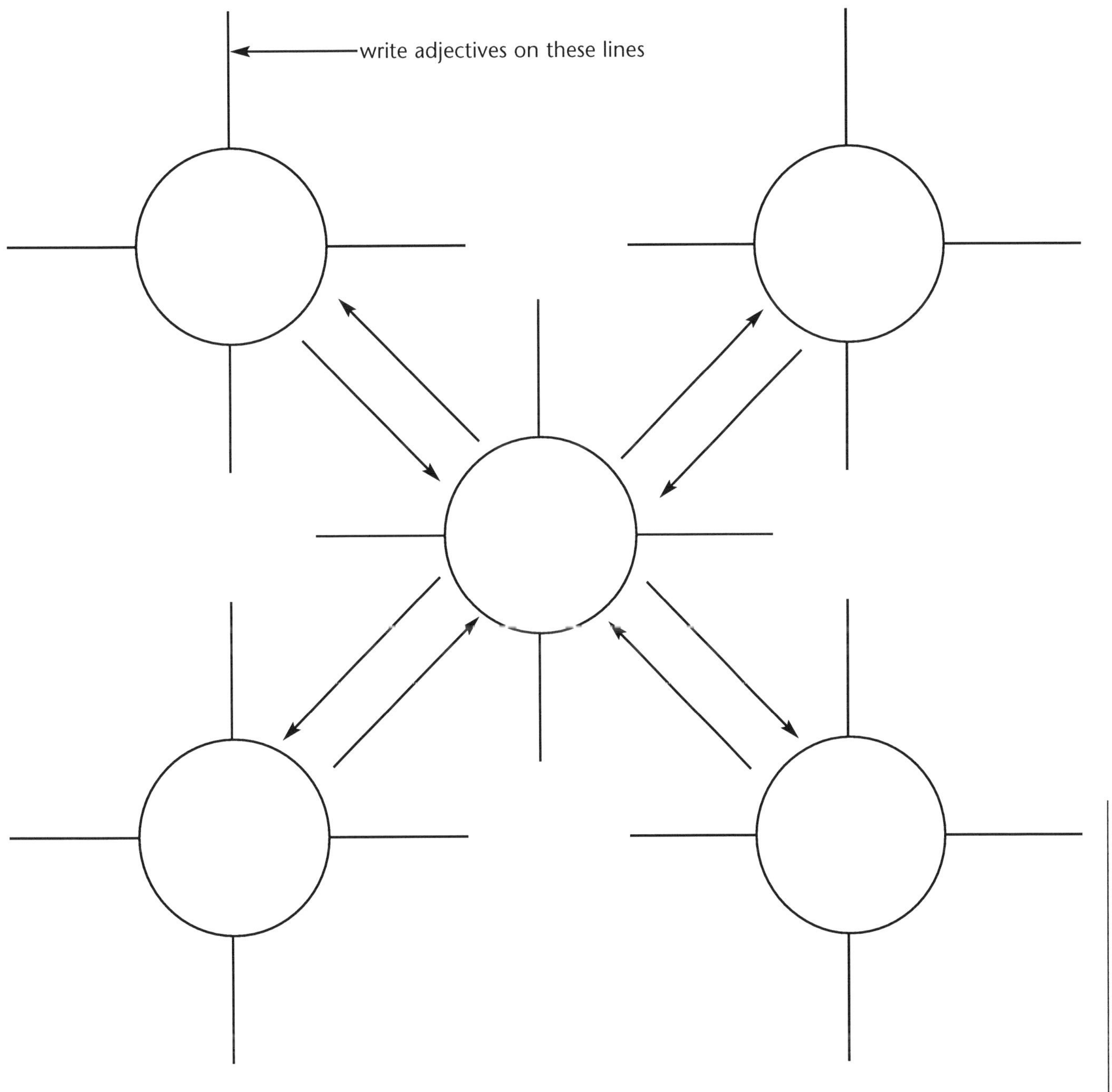

All rights reserved

Story Map

Characters____________________________________

Setting

Time and Place________________________________

Problem

Problem____________________________________

Goal

Goal______________________________________

Episodes

Beginning → Development → Outcome

Resolution

Resolution__________________________________

All rights reserved

 © Novel Units, Inc.

Sequence

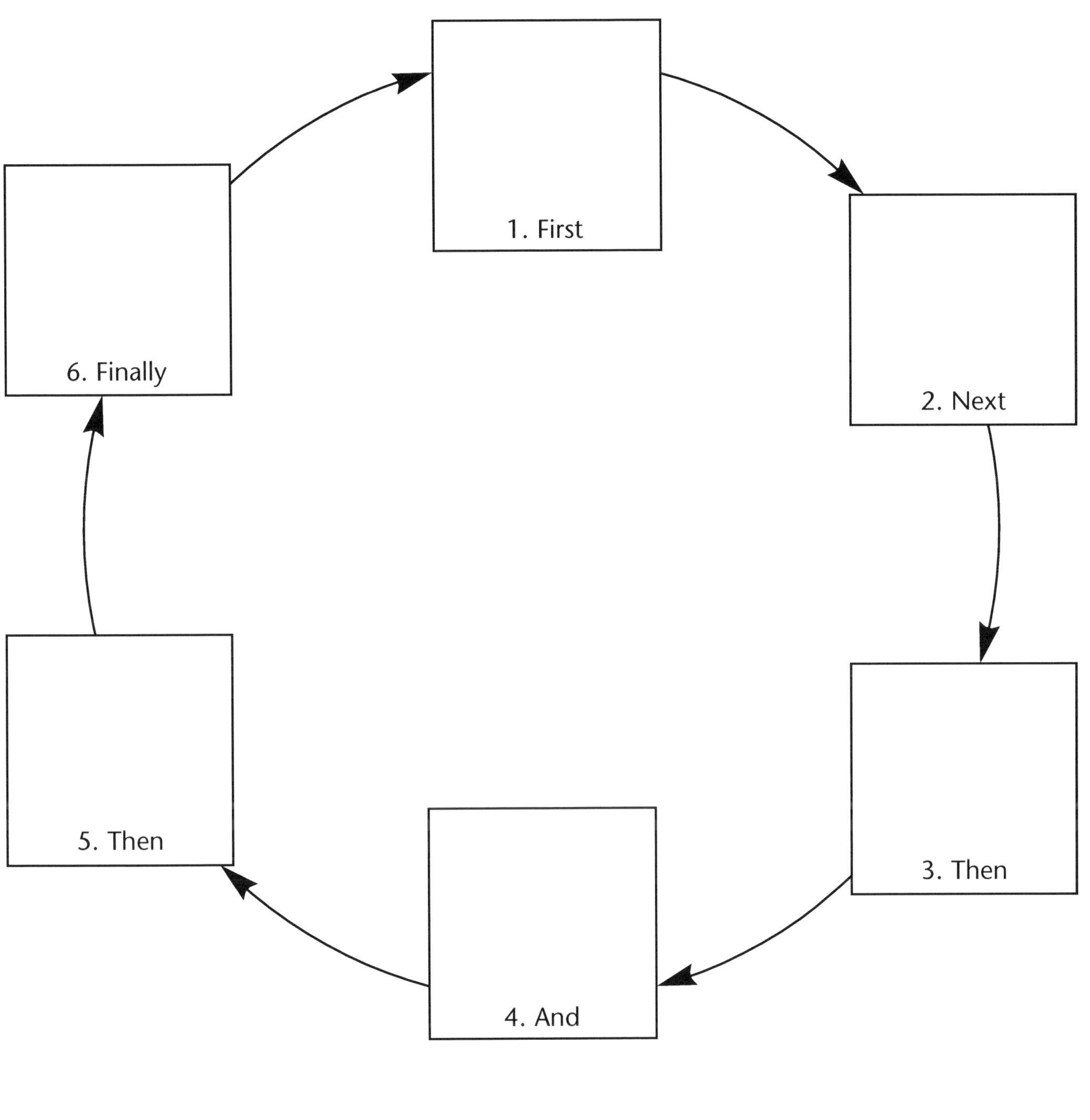

All rights reserved

Venn Diagram

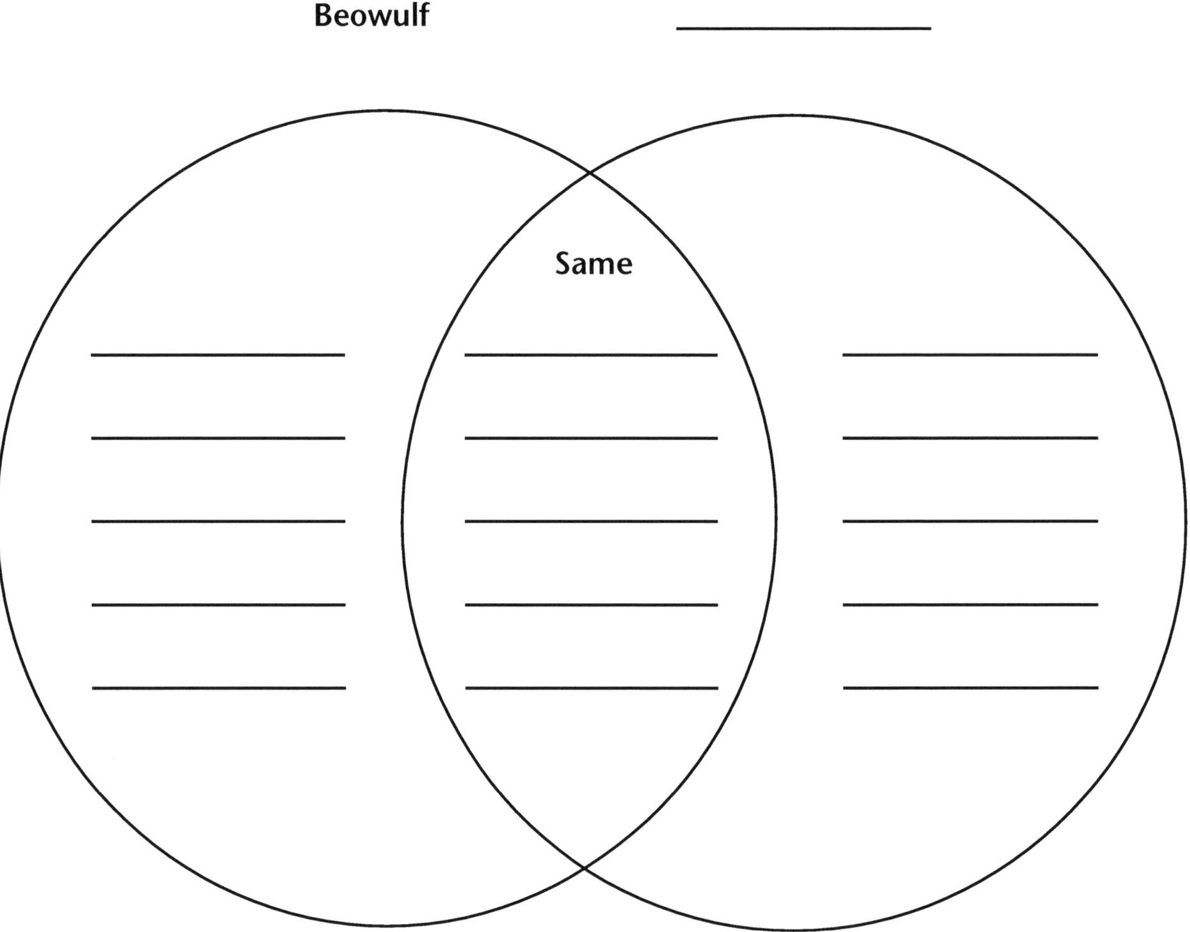

All rights reserved

 © Novel Units, Inc.

Note: Examples of similes, metaphors, and kennings found in each section are included in the Supplementary Activities. Guide students to identify these devices and the use of alliteration and caesura (see pages *xxviii-xxix*) as they read the novel. If students have their own books, have them underline examples of alliteration and mark examples of caesuras. Use an overhead transparency of the Foreshadowing Chart on page 7 of this guide to list foreshadowing clues as they occur in the poem. Guide students as they identify the occurrence of the foreshadowed event.

Lines 1–319, pp. 3–23

The Danes' King Hrothgar, of the lineage of Shield Sheafson, builds Heorot, a hall for his thanes. Grendel wreaks havoc on Hrothgar's men. After hearing of Grendel's destruction, Beowulf sails from Geatland to defend the Danes.

Vocabulary
foundling (3)
torques (7)
anathema (9)
wassail (11)
parley (13)
rabid (13)
thane (15)
interlopers (19)
mongering (21)

Discussion Questions

1. Discuss the information about Shield Sheafson and his lineage. Analyze the statement, "Behavior that's admired is the path to power among people everywhere" (p. 5) in conjunction with Sheafson's lineage. Ascertain the validity of this exhortation in today's world. *(Sheafson overcomes his beginning as a foundling to become a powerful, good king who conquers the foes of his people. His son, Beow, becomes renowned as a young prince who inspires enduring loyalty and later gains recognition as a well-regarded king. His heir, Halfdane, also becomes a notable king. Halfdane's son, Hrothgar, rules wisely, develops a mighty army, and builds a hall, Heorot, for his men. At Heorot, they feast, listen to a skilled poet recite the story of creation, and receive rewards each night. Because the prudent behavior of Sheafson, Beow, Halfdane, and Hrothgar promotes admiration and loyalty among their followers, each of the kings becomes powerful and wealthy. Responses will vary. pp. 3–9)*

2. Examine the data about Grendel: his origin, what incites him to violence against Hrothgar's kingdom, and his effect on the kingdom. *(Grendel is a demon from the family tree of Cain, who killed his brother Abel and became an outcast, producing a line of demons and giants. Grendel becomes enraged when he hears joyful sounds from Heorot. He listens to the poet telling the story of creation by an Almighty God, the same God who outlawed Cain, the patriarch of his clan. He attacks at night, initially killing thirty of Hrothgar's thanes. He continues his onslaught for twelve years, refusing to negotiate with Hrothgar, causing Heorot to stand empty and deserted, and haunting the hall at night. Hrothgar's kingdom is in chaos, riveted by terror and uncertainty. Hrothgar's counselors resort to pagan rituals in an attempt to defeat Grendel. pp. 9–13)*

3. Analyze why Grendel does not take over Hrothgar's throne. *(God protects the throne. Hrothgar's reign symbolizes good, e.g., he acknowledges the Almighty God. The demon Grendel, a descendant of the first murderer, symbolizes evil. p. 13)*

4. Examine the introduction of the Geat warrior into the plot. Analyze his heroic characteristics. *(He is a powerful man of noble lineage and is noted as the mightiest man on earth. Heroic qualities: responds to the need of others; is able to enlist the best men to accompany him; has the appearance of a valiant, adventurous man; fulfills obligations; speaks eloquently; offers his help and counsel. pp. 15–21)*

All rights reserved

5. Discuss the watchman's reaction to the arrival of the Geats and what this reveals about the Shieldings. *(The watchman carefully guards the Danish sea-cliffs against intruders. He demands to know why the Geats have come, and after hearing their leader's explanation, he undauntedly offers to escort them inland. Before leaving them, he invokes God's blessings. The Shieldings, under King Hrothgar, are cautious and alert to the possibility of enemy invaders. They reflect their leader's courage and honor. They primarily adhere to the tenets of Christianity. pp. 17–23)*

Supplementary Activities

1. Have students research burial rites for eighth-century Scandinavian kings and participate in an oral discussion correlating Shield Sheafson's burial with historical facts.
2. Have students list three kennings and identify what they metaphorically describe, then add three kennings for each section throughout the book.
3. Literary Devices: **Metaphor**—sun/moon: lamplight/lantern (p. 9) **Simile**—"...she (the ship) flew like a bird." (p. 17) **Kennings**—scourge of many tribes, wrecker of mead-benches, terror of the hall-troops: Shield Sheafson, whale-road: ocean (p. 3); ring-giver: Sheafson (p. 5); hall-watcher, death-shadow: Grendel (pp. 11, 13); treasure-seat: throne (p. 13); word-hoard: vocabulary (p. 19)

Lines 320–661, pp. 23–45

Hrothgar recognizes Beowulf's name and welcomes him. Beowulf vows to fight Grendel. Beowulf defends himself against Unferth's verbal challenge. Queen Wealhtheow welcomes Beowulf.

Vocabulary
formidable (27)
lament (31)
brook (35)
pinioned (39)
mizzle (41)

Discussion Questions

1. Discuss the reception Beowulf and his warriors receive in Denmark. What does this reveal about the Geats and the Danes? *(Wulfgar, a warrior chief, questions them first and believes they have come because of their bravery. Beowulf, who has especially impressed Wulfgar, reveals his name and asks to see the king. Wulfgar advises Hrothgar to see them. Hrothgar recognizes Beowulf's name because he had known Beowulf's father, and has heard marvelous tales of his son's strength. He sends Wulfgar to get Beowulf and his men, emphasizing that they are welcome in Denmark. The Geats appear well-born and worthy of respect, they do not force their way into the kingdom, and have come only to help the Danes. The Danes are cautious but hospitable and are thankful for Beowulf's offer of help. pp. 23–27)*
2. Examine what Beowulf reveals about himself and his purpose in coming to Denmark. *(He reveals his kinship to Hygelac and tells Hrothgar about some of his exploits, e.g., he battled and bound five beasts, raided the trolls' domain and killed them, and avenged his own people against their enemies. After hearing of the death and destruction Grendel is causing, he has come to defend the Danes by fighting Grendel hand-to-hand, without weapons. He understands his fate if Grendel defeats him but is willing to risk his life and his honor in order to free the Danes from the terror. pp. 29–31)*
3. Analyze Hrothgar's reply to Beowulf and what this implies. *(He tells the story of a feud Beowulf's father began that caused the death of Heatholaf, a Wulfing. Hrothgar healed the feud by financially compensating the Wulfings. Beowulf's father, Ecgtheow, responded to Hrothgar's help by vowing his allegiance to him. Implication: Beowulf will repay Hrothgar for Ecgtheow's debt. pp. 31–33)*

All rights reserved

 © Novel Units, Inc.

4. Discuss Unferth's challenge to Beowulf's honor and Beowulf's response. Analyze what this reveals about both of them. *(Unferth relates his version of Beowulf's swimming match with Breca, telling the others that pride made the two men venture out too far. He declares that, although Beowulf contended for seven days, Breca won the contest. Unferth predicts that Beowulf will lose the battle with Grendel. Beowulf reveals that he and Breca, equally matched, struggled for five nights but were separated by strong waves. The ocean deposited him safely on the coast of Finland. Beowulf reminds Unferth that he has never faced and conquered danger on the battlefield, that he [Unferth] has killed his own kin, and that if he were as courageous as he proclaims, Grendel would never have gotten away with the atrocities he has committed against the Danes. Beowulf vows to kill Grendel. Unferth is jealous, spiteful, and arrogant. Beowulf is confident, brave, and resolute. pp. 35–41)*
5. Allegorical Focus: Examine evidence of the blending of paganism and Christianity in this section. *(Hrothgar believes that the Holy God has sent Beowulf to defend the Danes against Grendel. Beowulf says that he believes God will decide whether he or Grendel will die [Christianity], then states that fate will rule their destiny [paganism]. Hrothgar says that fate sweeps his guards into Grendel's clutches [paganism], but that God can halt the attacks [Christianity]. Beowulf alludes to the light from the east as a guarantee of God, then says that fate spares a man. Wealhtheow thanks God for granting her wish and sending Beowulf to deliver the Danes. pp. 23–45)*
6. Analyze Beowulf's boast to Wealhtheow, her response, and Hrothgar's parting words to Beowulf. *(Beowulf vows to fulfill his purpose of freeing the Danes from Grendel, or meet his death in the attempt. Wealhtheow is pleased with his boast. Hrothgar wishes Beowulf health and good luck and reveals his trust in him by giving him control over Heorot. He admonishes Beowulf to guard the hall diligently and beware of the enemy. He promises him anything he wants if he defeats Grendel. Beowulf is confident and committed; Wealhtheow is appreciative and hopeful; Hrothgar is expectant and trusting. pp. 43–45)*
7. **Prediction:** Will Beowulf be successful in his quest to defeat Grendel?

Supplementary Activities

1. Working in small groups, have students write the script and stage the various scenes in this section: the meeting between Wulfgar and Beowulf, the first meeting between Beowulf and Hrothgar, the confrontation between Unferth and Beowulf, Wealhtheow's arrival and interaction with Beowulf, the parting scene between Beowulf and Hrothgar.
2. Literary Devices: **Simile**—"...they (dead sea monsters) slopped and floated like the ocean's leavings." (p. 39) **Kennings**—giver of rings: King Hrothgar (p. 25); heaven's dome: sky (p. 29); sleep of the sword: death (p. 39); Victory-Shieldings: Hrothgar's warriors, treasure-giver: King Hrothgar (p. 41); dawn-light: sunrise, hall-warden: Beowulf (p. 45)

All rights reserved

Lines 662–1007, pp. 45–67

Grendel kills one of Beowulf's men. After a vicious battle, Beowulf defeats Grendel. The Danes celebrate, and Hrothgar thanks God for the victory. He adopts Beowulf as a "child of his heart."

Vocabulary

mettle (45)
bourne (47)
bane (49)
baleful (49)
canny (49)
ignominious (57)

Discussion Questions

1. Allegorical focus: Analyze Beowulf's faith in himself, his faith in God, and his belief in fate. *(He places complete trust in his strength and in God's favor. He believes himself to be as strong and dangerous as Grendel and plans to face him unarmed. Even though he is confident of his ability, he prays that the Divine Lord, in His wisdom, will grant victory to whichever side He chooses, proving that he also believes in fate. pp. 45–47)*
2. Allegorical focus: Analyze the metaphorical content in and the significance of the statement, "But the Lord was weaving a victory on His war-loom for the Weather-Geats" (p. 47). *(Metaphorically, God's divine plan is portrayed as a loom on which He weaves a picture of Beowulf's ensuing battle with Grendel, revealing Beowulf winning the victory for the Geats and the Danes. The statement is significant because the Geats, as they wait for Grendel's attack, reflect on the nightly deaths of the Danes. They do not believe Beowulf will defeat Grendel and fear none of them will return to their homeland. p. 47)*
3. Discuss Grendel's description and characterization, and examine what this reveals about him. Note the descriptive kennings. *(He is a powerful, God-cursed bane of the race of men. He is spurned and joyless, filled with rage and demonic glee, and maddened for blood. He hunts his prey at night, guided by a deadly light that flares from his eyes. The Danes view him as a cancerous curse who comes to terrorize and kill. Kennings: captain of evil, dread of the land, hell-serf. pp. 49–53)*
4. Discuss the details of Beowulf's battle with Grendel. Analyze what this battle reveals about Beowulf, Grendel, and the other Geats. *(Beowulf is strong and cautious, but Grendel's stealth and speed enable him to grab one of the Geats at the onset of the battle. He then raises his talon to attack Beowulf, but the warrior grabs him in a powerful armlock from which he cannot escape. The two warriors crash through Heorot, smashing benches and wrecking the hall. Grendel emits a horrible scream as Beowulf injures him. As the two struggle, the other Geat warriors attack Grendel with their swords, but Grendel is impervious to all harm from the cutting edge of every weapon. Grendel finally weakens, and Beowulf tears his shoulder, arm, and claw from him. Grendel retreats to his lair. Both Grendel and Beowulf are powerful warriors, they hate each other, and they will fight until one dies. Beowulf's warriors are valiant but helpless against Grendel's demonic supernatural power. The Christian influence of the poet implies that God allows Beowulf, symbolic of good, to defeat the evil Grendel because he has cursed God and is a servant of hell. pp. 51–57)*
5. Compare and contrast Beowulf with Sigemund and King Heremod. Discuss why you think these two tales are included. *(Sigemund is a hero of Norse mythology who killed a dragon and retrieved its treasure hoard. He was valiant and adventurous, and poets continue to sing his praises. He and Beowulf are comparable in their courage and their desire for adventure. The story of Sigemund foreshadows Beowulf's final battle with a dragon. King Heremod is a foil for both Beowulf and Hrothgar. His competence and leadership ability decline, he becomes a source of anxiety to his men, and he becomes evil. His warriors can no longer rely on him to defend the nation, and he finally dies in an ambush. Beowulf will continue to be a man of valor and will ultimately become a notable king. Hrothgar retains his leadership ability and integrity until his death. Both will die with honor. Responses will vary. pp. 59–61)*

All rights reserved

 © Novel Units, Inc.

6. Examine the aftermath of Grendel's defeat. *(The warriors gather to survey Grendel's bloody trail to his lair and the churning water of his "hell." They rejoice and laud Beowulf repeatedly, and a minstrel begins to sing his praises, comparing him to the dragon-slayer Sigemund. Hrothgar greets Beowulf at Heorot Hall. He views Grendel's claw and gives thanks to God for the victory. He praises Beowulf for his victory and adopts him in his heart as a son. Hrothgar promises Beowulf anything he desires, declares that his actions have made him immortal, and asks God to keep him well and safe. Beowulf responds with a description of the battle and the assurance that Grendel will die and face the judgment of God. Everyone works to repair Heorot. pp. 55–67)*
7. Allegorical focus: Analyze the names for the Christian God on page 63 of the novel. Share other names you have heard applied to other deities. *(Almighty Father, Heavenly Shepherd, Lord of Ages, God of Ages. Responses will vary.)*
8. **Prediction:** What will happen to Grendel?

Supplementary Activities

1. Have students do one of the following: (a) sketch Grendel (b) sketch Grendel's claw (c) write a metaphor or simile poem about valor (d) write a five-senses poem about "Terror."
2. Literary Devices: **Simile**—"Every nail, claw-scale and spur, every spike and welt...(on Grendel's hand)...was like barbed steel." (p. 65) **Kennings**—house-guard: the king's protectors, breast-mail: armor (p. 45); sea-rovers: Beowulf's companions (p. 47); guardian of the hoard: dragon (p. 59)

Lines 1007–1250, pp. 67–89

Hrothgar hosts a victory feast. He gives Beowulf lavish gifts and rewards the other warriors. The king's poet performs the tale of Hildeburh. Wealhtheow gives Beowulf a golden torque.

Vocabulary
carnage (69) coffer (69) bereft (71) keens (77) boons (83)

Discussion Questions

1. Discuss the mood in Heorot Hall during the victory celebration. Note the foreshadowing of future events in Hrothgar's kingdom. *(The hall is filled with famous men of the kingdom, and a light-hearted atmosphere of friendship and good will prevails. Hrothgar and Hrothulf, his nephew, are elated. The king rewards Beowulf and his men. Minstrels perform music and tales of adventure to please the hero. "The Shielding nation was not yet familiar with feud and betrayal" [p. 67] foreshadows eventual problems in Hrothgar's kingdom. Wealhtheow reminds Hrothgar of his responsibility to bequeath his kingdom to his own kin. Her discourse about Hrothulf's honor in treating Hrothgar's sons fairly foreshadows Hrothulf's eventual betrayal of the sons after Hrothgar's death. pp. 67–71, 83)*
2. Discuss the gifts Beowulf receives from Hrothgar and Wealhtheow and Beowulf's response to these gifts. Analyze the symbolism of each gift. *(The gifts: a gold flag—victory; armor—strength and protection; a sword—honor; eight horses—swiftness and power; gold—wealth and renown; a golden torque—luck. Beowulf is pleased with the gifts and sees no shame in being showered with such gifts in front of his men, knowing he deserves them because he has freed the kingdom from Grendel's evil. pp. 69, 85–87)*
3. Note the understatement in the opening lines of the story of Hildeburh. Discuss the tale's significance. The story, known as the "Finnsburg episode," is a poem-within-a-poem,

All rights reserved

indicated by the use of italics (p. *xiii*). *(Understatement: "Hildeburh had little cause to credit the Jutes" [p. 71]—she had abundant cause to discredit them. Because of them, she loses her son, her brother, and her husband. Significance: demonstrates an honor-bound, blood-stained society where vengeance is an integral duty of the heroic code. Hildeburh's story also illustrates the role of fate, an important component throughout the novel. pp. 71–81,* xiii-xiv*)*

4. Analyze the uniqueness of Hildeburh's role. Discuss the fates of the innocent victims of war, e.g., wives, mothers, children. *(The story implies that she left her own people to marry Finn as a peace-pledge between the Danes and the Frisians. She is caught in the conflict between the two countries and becomes a victim of circumstance who is left without a husband, son, or brother. Responses will vary. pp. 71–81)*

5. Examine the effects of the war. Discuss the terms of the truce between Hengest and Finn and why it failed. Compare the Danes with exiled soldiers in 20th and 21st century wars. *(The Danes agree to a truce after their indecisive attack against the Frisians. The Danes are to have separate quarters and share the mead-hall with the Frisians. Finn is to give equal gifts to the Danes and his own warriors. Finn guarantees the Danes honor and status and vows that his men will not provoke the Danes. Icy, stormy conditions prevent the Danes from returning home during the winter, and they become homesick, resentful, and sullen. When spring arrives, old accusations against Finn erupt, and Hengest leads a revolt against Finn, killing him in his home. Responses will vary. pp. 73–81)*

6. Discuss the golden torque Beowulf receives: what eventually happens to it, what this foreshadows, and Wealhtheow's parting words to Beowulf. *(The torque is a resplendent necklace of gold. Beowulf will eventually give the torque to King Hygelac, who is wearing it when he is killed in battle against the Frisians. They take the torque as a trophy of war. Wealhtheow tells Beowulf to wear the torque and the armor for luck. She wishes him a lifetime of luck and asks him to treat her sons kindly. Her request that Beowulf treat her sons with tender care signifies her premonition that something will happen to them after Hrothgar's death. pp. 85–87)*

7. **Prediction**: What threat looms over the thanes as they retire for the night? Why is one of the warriors marked for death?

Supplementary Activities

1. Working in small groups, have students research current efforts at developing a truce between two groups of people, e.g. Israelis/Palestinians. Have them participate in an oral discussion comparing the success of these efforts with the truce between the Danes and the Frisians and discuss what they think are the components of a lasting and effective truce.

2. Have a volunteer sketch his or her impression of the golden torque Wealhtheow gives Beowulf.

3. Literary Devices: **Kennings**—sea-lanes: ocean (p. 81); neck-chain, neck-ring, neck-torque: necklace (p. 85); war-helmet, mail-shirt: armor (p. 87)

All rights reserved

© Novel Units, Inc.

Lines 1251–1491, pp. 89–103

Grendel's mother arrives at Heorot to avenge her son's death. She seizes Hrothgar's close friend Aeschere and retrieves Grendel's hand.

Vocabulary

sallied (89)
depredations (93)
mere (95)
hart (95)
scud (97)
bulwark (97)
screes (99)
tempered (101)

Discussion Questions

1. Analyze the reappearance of evil and its effect in Heorot and on Hrothgar. *(Grendel's mother comes to Heorot to avenge her son's death. She enters Heorot but panics when the thanes begin to attack her. Before fleeing, she snatches Grendel's hand and Aeschere, one of Hrothgar's most loved and trusted warriors. Heorot is in an uproar and Hrothgar is grief-stricken. Beowulf, who had lodged elsewhere for the night, returns. pp. 89–93)*
2. Analyze the kennings that characterize Grendel's mother. *(Kennings: monstrous hell-bride, hell-dam, roaming killer, troll-dam. She is of the evil lineage of Cain, the first murderer. An atrocious bride of perdition, she gave birth to the demon Grendel. "Dam" indicates that she is an animal's mother, e.g., Grendel's vicious, animal-like actions. She is the parental role model for Grendel. Note lines 1353–1357, which allude to Grendel's unnatural birth and characterize him and his mother as "fatherless creatures" with an ancestry of demons and ghosts. Although she symbolizes evil, her actions as a mother avenging her son's death are appropriate for this era of vengeance. pp. 89–95)*
3. Discuss the country people's tales about the monsters, and examine their effect on the Danes. *(The poet describes two creatures from another world that prowl the moors and raid the countryside. One looks like a woman, and the other is in the shape of a man, yet is larger than any man. Nothing is known of a father, and although their past is hidden, they are of a lineage of demons and ghosts. They live among the wolves in the hills and often inhabit a haunted lake, where the water burns and writhes and even the deer willingly face death from pursuing hounds rather than dive into its depths. No human has ever explored the depths of the lake. The Danes are terror-stricken, and Hrothgar believes Beowulf is the only one who can find and destroy Grendel's mother. pp. 95–97)*
4. Analyze the symbolism of the terrain and the creatures in the lake where Grendel's mother dwells. *(The woods in the moor are dark and dismal. Ledges of cliffs with mazes of tree roots lie above bloodshot water lairs of monsters. The hot, gory water is infested with all kinds of reptiles. Monsters and sea-dragons slouch on the slopes of the cliffs surrounding the lake. Each part of the terrain and each creature attest to the foreboding, evil influence of Grendel and his mother and symbolize the hell from which they originally came. pp. 95–99)*
5. Examine the heroic code by which Beowulf lives as revealed in his response to Hrothgar's plea for help. *(Beowulf believes it is better to avenge loved ones than to engage in mourning. Knowing that death is certain some day, a warrior must do what he can to win glory before death because only those deeds he does before death will be remembered. Beowulf wants to waste no time in pursuing Grendel's mother and encourages Hrothgar to accept and endure his troubles and become the man everyone expects him to be. p. 97)*
6. Discuss Beowulf's preparations for the battle with Grendel's mother. Examine Unferth's role and what this reveals about him. *(Beowulf puts on his armor to protect his body and a helmet to guard his head. Unferth, knowing he is not man enough to face Grendel's mother himself, gives Beowulf his sword, which is called Hrunting. Beowulf takes this sword, which has never failed its user in any battle and has been utilized to perform heroic deeds, into battle. pp. 101–103)*

All rights reserved

7. Analyze what Beowulf's parting speech to Hrothgar reveals about both of them. (*Beowulf alludes to the possibility of his death. He asks Hrothgar to take care of the young Geats who have come with him and to send the treasures he has received to Hygelac. He wants Unferth to receive the sword. Beowulf recognizes Hrothgar as a wise king and believes he meant it when he said he would adopt him as a son of his heart. He wants Hygelac to perceive the greatness of Hrothgar by seeing the symbols of appreciation he received for slaying Grendel. Beowulf is a man of honor who is concerned about his men, his king, and Unferth. p. 103*)
8. **Prediction**: What will be the outcome of Beowulf's confrontation with Grendel's mother?

Supplementary Activities

1. Have a volunteer sketch Hrunting.
2. Working in small groups, have students create a collage that depicts the evil of Grendel and his mother.
3. Literary Devices: **Kennings**—gold-hall: Heorot, hell-brute: Grendel, death-den: Grendel's lair (p. 89); Shieldings' helmet: King Hrothgar, soul-mate: Aeschere (p. 93); gap of danger: Grendel's mother's lair (p. 97); water-monsters: reptiles (p. 99); boar-spears: arrows (p. 101); gold-friend: King Hrothgar (p. 103)

Lines 1492–1887, pp. 103–129

Beowulf dives into the lake where Grendel's mother lives. She captures him, but he eventually overpowers and beheads her with an ancient sword. He carries her head to Heorot. Hrothgar admonishes Beowulf to avoid pride and beware of life's fragility. The Geats feast and rest before returning home.

Vocabulary
sage (111)
fettle (113)
tender (115)
damascened (115)
venerable (115)
pariah (119)
felicity (119)
overweening (119)
alacrity (125)
gannet (127)
whorled (127)
peerless (129)

Discussion Questions

1. Contrast the details of these two events: Beowulf's battle with Grendel's mother and his fight with Grendel. Analyze Beowulf's superhuman characteristics and the providential help he receives. *(Contrast: Beowulf fought Grendel in familiar territory, i.e., a mead-hall. Grendel had no one to help him. Beowulf fights Grendel's mother in the dark, alien waters of her lair, where her protectors, i.e., the sea-monsters, attack him. Beowulf's superhuman characteristics: his ability to stay under water for a long period of time and his superior ability to swim; his strength to lift and wield the giant's sword. Providential help: the Holy God decides the victory by enabling Beowulf to recover from the initial attack and to see the giant's sword. pp. 103–115)*
2. Analyze the imagery of darkness and light in the battle scene. *(Darkness symbolizes evil; light symbolizes goodness. Beowulf must fight Grendel's mother in the darkness of her own territory, a world with which he is unfamiliar and in which he is at first ineffective. The first gleam of light he observes comes from firelight in the depths of the lake, allowing him to see the demon. Immediately after Beowulf kills Grendel's mother, light appears and the place brightens as if the sun is shining. Allegorical focus: The lake symbolizes hell, and when Beowulf purges the evil demon, the light of God's purity invades the darkness. pp. 105–109)*

All rights reserved

3. Analyze the effects of the triumph of good over evil. *(Light pierces the darkness, the scalding blood of Grendel's mother causes the sword blade to melt, the reptiles flee from the lake, and the lake settles as clouds darken above. The light returns, the sword blade will no longer destroy the innocent, and the lake returns to normal. pp. 109–113)*
4. Discuss the reactions of the men who wait for Beowulf to return. Allegorical Focus: Note the reference to the ninth hour. *(They see the surge of bloody water from the lake and believe Grendel's mother has killed Beowulf. The ninth hour symbolizes the time of Christ's death on the cross [Bible, Matthew 27:45–46]. At the ninth hour, the hopeless warriors abandon their lookout post, and the king goes home, thinking evil has conquered. pp. 109–111)*
5. Analyze the importance of the sword hilt Beowulf gives Hrothgar. Note that the engraving on the hilt correlates with the Biblical account of the flood in Genesis 6–7. *(The sword hilt is an ancient relic, and the poet infers it once belonged to the giants of Genesis 6:4. The engraving tells of the first war and the flood that destroyed the giants. This section reflects that the Anglo-Saxons had access to stories from the Bible in the mid-700s. pp. 115–117)*
6. Analyze Hrothgar's discourse on the dangers of power and the importance of the story of Heremod. *(Hrothgar first affirms Beowulf as a man born to distinction whose fame has spread widely. He praises Beowulf as a man who is even-tempered, prudent, and resolute, and he renews his vow of friendship. He prophesies Beowulf's importance in his own kingdom. In the midst of Hrothgar's oratory, he introduces the story of Heremod, a foil for Beowulf. Heremod was an evil king who became enraged and killed his own men, rebelled against God, became bloodthirsty for more power, and lost all happiness. Hrothgar tells Beowulf that God may grant him power but cautions him that allowing pride to control him will result in covetousness, resentment, and dishonor. At his death, his possessions will belong to someone else. He encourages Beowulf to choose eternal rewards rather than temporal rewards. Hrothgar closes his discourse by relating his own belief that he had purged his country of its enemies only to have Grendel appear and by praising God for the victory. pp. 117–123)*
7. Discuss the farewells between Hrothgar and Beowulf. Note the foreshadowing in Hrothgar's final words, lines 1840–1865. *(Beowulf and his men are anxious to return to their own country. Beowulf thanks Hrothgar for treating them well and pledges his help for the Danes if they are ever threatened by attacks from other countries. He reveals his confidence in Hygelac's support should he need to return to Denmark. Hrothgar commends Beowulf for his strength and maturity and for drawing the Geats and the Danes into a shared peace and friendship. He tells Beowulf that, if Hygelac dies, he has the ability to become a powerful king of the Geats. He gives Beowulf farewell gifts, then breaks into tears as he tells him good-bye, knowing they will never meet again. Hrothgar's final words foreshadow Hygelac's death and Beowulf's ascension to the throne in Geatland. pp. 125–129)*
8. **Prediction**: What awaits the Geats when they return home?

Supplementary Activities

1. Have students work with a partner and write a five-senses poem about "Pride" based on King Hrothgar's discourse. Share the poems with the class.
2. Literary Devices: **Metaphor**—arrow: pride (p. 121) **Simile**—"...it (sword) melted as ice melts..." (p. 111) **Kennings**—swamp-thing from hell, tarn-hag: Grendel's mother (p. 105); house of her flesh: Grendel's mother's head, heaven's candle: sun/moon (p. 109); seafarers' leader: Beowulf (p. 113); soul's guard: conscience (p. 119); heaven's joy: morning sun (p. 123)

All rights reserved

Lines 1888–2199, pp. 129–149

Beowulf and his men return to Geatland, where King Hygelac welcomes them warmly. Beowulf tells of his adventures in Denmark and presents his gifts to Hygelac and Hygd. Hygelac then rewards Beowulf.

Vocabulary

offing (131)
ensconced (131)
maw (141)
accoutrement (143)
scion (147)

Discussion Questions

1. Discuss Beowulf's arrival in Geatland and his reception by King Hygelac. *(The harbor guard has watched diligently for the arrival of his friends and hurries to meet them. King Hygelac and Queen Hygd welcome them to Hygelac's mead-hall. Hygelac questions Beowulf about his voyage and whether or not he helped Hrothgar. Beowulf describes the battles with Grendel and his mother and relates information about Hrothgar and his family. He tells of the honor and riches he received from Hrothgar, then presents his gifts to Hygelac and Hygd. As Beowulf tells the story of his victories over the evil demons, the Geats reverse their prior opinion that Beowulf was a weakling. Hygelac presents Beowulf with an heirloom sword, livestock, land, a hall, and a throne. Beowulf's homecoming and his warm reception from Hygelac deepen their respect for and devotion to each other. pp. 131–149)*

2. Analyze the poet's rationale for including the story of the evil Queen Modthryth. *(Queen Modthryth serves as a foil to Hygd, queen of Geatland, and to Wealhtheow, queen of the Danes. Both Hygd and Wealhtheow are gracious and kind, faithful to their husbands, and attentive to their husband's thanes. They both promote peace in their kingdoms and with other nations. Modthryth was cruel and vicious, often having men tortured and put to death for imagined insults or attempts at seduction. Even her beauty could not compensate for her brutality. Her marriage to Offa transformed her into a devoted wife who was known for her good deeds. pp. 133–135)*

3. Discuss evidence of Beowulf's loyalty to his king and queen and examine the attributes that make him a classic hero. *(Beowulf tells Hygelac that his victory over Grendel won credit for his king and his people. He acknowledges Hygelac as the one on whom he depends for favor and pays homage to Hygelac and Hygd by giving them the gifts he received from Hrothgar. He presents the flag, helmet, armor, sword, and four horses to Hygelac. To Hygd, he gives the golden necklace and three horses. Attributes of a classic hero displayed by Beowulf include his valor, his capacity to keep his temper, and his ability to guard and control his natural strength. He never takes advantage of a comrade, and although formidable in battle, he always behaves honorably. pp. 143, 149)*

4. Analyze Beowulf's prophecy concerning a peace-pledge marriage. Participate in a class discussion concerning arranged marriages. *(In telling Hygelac about the Danes, Beowulf alludes to the proposed marriage of Hrothgar's daughter, Freawaru. Hrothgar hopes her marriage to Ingeld, a Heathobard, will promote peace between the two nations. Beowulf predicts the wedding will trigger memories of the Heathobards' deaths and defeat at the hands of the Danes. When the Heathobards see the Danes wearing armor they looted from the Heathobards and recall the massacre, fierce fighting will erupt and break the peace between the two nations. Note that Wealhtheow is also a peace-pledge between nations, lines 2016–2017. pp. 137–139)*

5. Identify examples of Beowulf's belief in fate. (*He attributes the death of Handscio, the Geat that Grendel killed, to fate. In his battle with Grendel's mother, he says he managed to escape with his life because his time had not yet come. pp. 141, 145*)

6. **Prediction**: What will Beowulf's role be in Hygelac's kingdom?

All rights reserved

Supplementary Activities

1. Have students analyze lines 2005–2009, i.e., references to Grendel's offspring, then write a paragraph in which they state whether they do or do not think the deaths of Grendel and his mother have ended their reign of evil.
2. Literary Devices: **Simile**—"...mail-shirt grey as hoar-frost..." (p. 147) **Kenning**—heaven's gem: sun (p. 141)

Lines 2200–2537, pp. 149–171

King Hygelac is killed in battle. Beowulf supports Hygelac's son and heir, Heardred, who also dies. Beowulf becomes king and rules well for fifty years. A dragon wreaks havoc on the Geats, and Beowulf prepares to fight the dragon. Flashbacks reveal information about Hygelac's death, the ensuing reign and death of Herebeald, and Beowulf's ascension to the throne.

Vocabulary
barrow (151)
trove (151)
pillage (155)
harrower (155)
gloaming (157)
linden (159)
prodigious (161)
reconnoitre (163)
wean (165)
redress (165)
quarter (167)
mercenary (169)

Discussion Questions

1. Discuss the circumstances that lead to Beowulf becoming king of the Geats, and examine examples of Beowulf's honor. Have students note the flashback on pages 159–163, and examine why the poet inserts this section in the tale of the dragon. *(Hygelac dies in the conflict against the Shylfings in Friesland. Beowulf escapes because of his superhuman swimming ability. Queen Hygd offers him the throne, but Beowulf chooses to support Hygelac's son Heardred in the role. After Heardred dies in a feud with the Swedes, Beowulf ascends to the throne and reigns for fifty years. Examples of his honor include his allegiance to Heardred as long as he lives and his avenging Heardred by killing Onela. This section contrasts the vigor of the young Beowulf in earlier battles with the declining strength of the older Beowulf in his fight with the dragon. pp. 149–151, 159–163)*
2. Examine the details leading to the dragon's attack on the Geats. Analyze instances in which one person can have a damaging effect on many others. *(A Geat slave fleeing from a cruel master inadvertently finds the dragon's treasure hoard and takes a goblet. The dragon becomes enraged and begins to terrorize the Geats by burning their homes and scorching their land. He eventually burns Beowulf's own home. Responses will vary. pp. 151–155)*
3. Analyze why the original owner of the treasure hid it, and discuss how the dragon got it. What "tales" do you think the treasure could relate? *(The lone survivor of a high-born forgotten race, knowing that he would soon die, buried his people's treasure. War had destroyed his people, and the honorable men who earned the treasure would never need it again. He had no one left with whom to share his life, and he mournfully roamed the earth until he died. The dragon accidentally found the treasure and has guarded it for three hundred years. Responses will vary. pp. 153–155)*
4. Examine Beowulf's preparation for his conflict with the dragon and why he is confident of victory. Note the foreshadowing of the deaths of both Beowulf and the dragon. *(Beowulf takes twelve men with him to search for the dragon's lair, including the thief who stole the goblet. He is confident of victory because he has survived many prior perils and ordeals since the time he defeated Grendel and his mother. He believes he will defeat the dragon, but he also senses his own approaching death. He takes his sword, wears armor and a helmet, and carries a shield as*

All rights reserved

protection against the dragon's fiery breath. pp. 159, 165, 169–171 Foreshadowing: lines 2342–2344, 2420–2424)

5. Discuss the recapitulation of Beowulf's early days in King Hrethel's court. Examine the circumstances leading to Herebeald's death and why Hrethel failed to seek revenge according to the law of the blood-feud. Discuss the universality of grief. *(Beowulf becomes a ward of Hrethel when he is seven years old. Hrethel treats Beowulf as well as he does his own three sons, Herebeald, Haethcyn, and Hygelac. Haethcyn accidentally kills Herebeald with a bow and arrow. Hrethel cannot avenge one son by the death of another, although he no longer loves Haethcyn. Hrethel's grief causes him to lose all interest in life and eventually leads to his death. Responses will vary. pp. 165–167)*
6. Discuss Beowulf's final address to his companions and analyze why he resolves to fight the dragon alone. *(Beowulf tells them he would prefer to fight the dragon without a weapon but knows he must protect himself. He vows he will not retreat from the dragon and will win or die. He believes fate will decide the outcome. He asks his men to remain safe on the barrow and resolves to fight the dragon alone because the fight is his alone. He is too proud to take others with him [see p. 159] and believes his courage will sustain him. p. 171)*
7. **Prediction**: What will be the outcome of Beowulf's confrontation with the dragon?

Supplementary Activities

1. Have students bring to class pictures or sketches of dragons. Prepare a classroom montage of these pictures.
2. Literary Devices: **Kennings**—earth-house: dragon's lair (p. 151); hoard-watcher, sky-winger: dragon (p. 157); throne-room: Beowulf's palace, hall-troop: Beowulf's men, sky-plague: dragon (p. 159); earth-vault: dragon's lair (p. 163)

Lines 2538–2820, pp. 171–191

After three intense battles, Beowulf kills the dragon but dies from its venomous bite. Only Wiglaf remains with and assists Beowulf. Wiglaf retrieves treasure from the dragon's lair and carries it to Beowulf. Just before he dies, Beowulf gives Wiglaf his golden necklace.

Vocabulary
foiled (175)
suppurating (183)
rampart (183)
fomented (185)
filigree (187)
pyre (189)

Discussion Questions

1. Analyze the symbolism of the dragon, Beowulf, and Wiglaf. Note the reference to fate. *(The dragon symbolizes the potent evil that invades Geatland. Beowulf symbolizes the virtue that can conquer evil. Wiglaf symbolizes the "passing of the torch" to another who will seek to eradicate evil as Beowulf has done. Lines 2573–2574: For the first time, fate denies Beowulf in this final battle. pp. 171–183)*
2. Examine Wiglaf's rationale for staying with Beowulf, and discuss his speech to the deserters. Evaluate Wiglaf's role. *(Wiglaf reminds the men of their pledges of loyalty to Beowulf when times were good in the mead-hall, tells them Beowulf chose them because they were the best of his thanes, and speaks of Beowulf's goodness to them. He pleads for unity and urges them to support Beowulf in this hour of need. Wiglaf stays with Beowulf because he adheres to the heroic code just as his king has always done. He demonstrates his moral strength, courage, and loyalty by fulfilling his vow to the king.*

All rights reserved

Wiglaf symbolizes the continuance of Beowulf's legacy, i.e., Beowulf takes the collar of gold from his own neck and gives it to Wiglaf, then tells him that he is the only one left of Beowulf's high-born clan. pp. 177–179, 189)

3. Analyze Beowulf's summation of his life and correlate this with the heroic code. *(He reflects back on his fifty years as king, referring to the courage and strength with which he defended his kingdom. He believes he has lived according to God's laws and can now face the "Ruler of mankind" blamelessly. Heroic code: ruled wisely, protected and cared for his people, accepted what came without complaint, never evoked quarrels, never swore to a lie. p. 185)*
4. Discuss why Beowulf asks Wiglaf to bring him some of the dragon's treasure and what Wiglaf finds. *(Beowulf wants to see the ancient treasure he has died to retrieve. The treasure will be his legacy to his own people. He has not been fortunate to have a son, and his people have filled that void for him. Wiglaf discovers gold goblets and vessels, a gold banner, and rusted armor. pp. 185–187)*
5. Examine Beowulf's final request. Why do you think Beowulf makes this request? *(He asks Wiglaf to order his troops to construct a barrow to be known as "Beowulf's Barrow" on a cliff overlooking the sea as a lasting memorial to his legacy as the king of the Geats. Responses will vary. p. 189)*

Supplementary Activities

1. Working in small groups, have students write a movie script for the battle between Beowulf and the dragon. The script should include the titles of appropriate background music, lighting directions, instructions for the cameraman, and speaking parts for Beowulf, the dragon, and Wiglaf.
2. Literary Devices: **Kennings**—rock-face: mountain side (p. 173); mound-keeper: dragon, battle-fire: dragon's breath (p. 175); ground-burner: dragon (p. 183); breast-cage: chest (p. 189)

Lines 2821–3182, pp. 191–213

The men who deserted Beowulf return. Wiglaf rebukes them, reveals details of Geat history, and predicts a tragic future for the Geats. Beowulf's body is burned on a funeral pyre, and his people build a memorial barrow for him.

Vocabulary
disdainfully (193) wake (197) rout (197) swathe (199) graith (201) gainsaying (201) dirges (213)

Discussion Questions

1. Discuss the return of the deserters and examine Wiglaf's rebuke. Allegorical focus: Note the reference to the providence of God. *(The deserters are ashamed and return behind their shields to where Beowulf lies dead and where Wiglaf tries vainly to revive him. In his rebuke, Wiglaf shames the men who ran away, reminds them of Beowulf's goodness toward them, and predicts that their cowardice will bring disaster when other nations hear of their desertion of their king. He sends a messenger to tell Beowulf's people of his death. Providence: Wiglaf cannot alter God's will; God ordains who wins or loses and had allowed Beowulf to strike the dragon at the correct time. pp. 193–195)*

All rights reserved

2. Analyze the prophecies concerning the Geat kingdom. Discuss the information about the Geats' wars with their enemies. Note prior references to the nations mentioned in the prophecy. *(A messenger predicts wars with the Franks, the Frisians [pp. 71–81], and a revival of a long-standing feud with the Swedes [pp. 161–169]. He refers to prior conflicts when Hygelac was king and foresees retaliation against the Geats now that Beowulf, who had kept the kingdom safe, is dead. He ends his prophecy by warning of exile and tragedy in the Geats' future. A Geat woman, while mourning at Beowulf's funeral pyre, prophesies invasion of their nation, enemies on the rampage, piles of bodies, slavery, and degradation. pp. 195–203, 211)*

3. Analyze the irony of the dragon's treasure, and discuss its disposal. *(The gold objects are tarnished and corroded and the armor, containers, and swords have rusted. The dragon has guarded a treasure for 300 years which was under a spell. Under the curse, whoever stole it would be guilty of wrong-doing and would be punished. The treasure thus brings death to both the dragon and Beowulf. Wiglaf takes the others to view the dragon's hoard. They load the treasure on a cart, and then bury it in Beowulf's Barrow. pp. 205–207, 213)*

4. Evaluate Wiglaf's reflections on Beowulf's fate and the finalization of Beowulf's request. *(Wiglaf believes Beowulf followed his own will in spite of admonitions from his advisors not to anger the dragon, and that many will be hurt because of his actions. He views Beowulf's death as a cruel fate. Wiglaf gives the orders for building Beowulf's funeral pyre. The Geat people hang helmets, armor, and shields on the pyre, build a huge fire, and burn Beowulf's body. The people mourn disconsolately. They build a barrow as Beowulf had requested, and place anything left from the fire inside it, including the dragon's treasure. Twelve warriors ride around the tomb, chanting dirges praising Beowulf's heroism, giving thanks for his greatness, and acclaiming him as the kindest, most famous king on the earth. pp. 207–213)*

Supplementary Activities

1. Have students write a funeral dirge for Beowulf.
2. Literary Devices: **Kennings**—sky-roamer, barrow-dweller: dragon, treasure-lodge: dragon's lair (p. 191); battle-dodgers, tail-turners: deserters (p. 193); steel-hail: battle, shield-wall: armor (p. 209); bone-house: funeral pyre (p. 211)

All rights reserved

Post–reading Discussion Questions

1. Using the Foreshadowing Chart on page 7 of this guide, discuss examples of foreshadowing throughout the book. *(Beowulf's swimming match with Breca—Beowulf's ability to fight Grendel's mother underwater and to escape by swimming to safety after Hygelac is killed. References to Hrothgar's sons and Hrothulf during the victory celebration after Grendel's death—Hrothulf's eventual betrayal of the sons. Wealhtheow's request that Beowulf treat her sons kindly—her premonition that something will happen to them after Hrothgar's death. The story of Heremod and Hrothgar's parting words to Beowulf—Hygelac's death and Beowulf's ascension to the Geat throne. The legend of Sigemund—Beowulf's fight with the dragon.)*
2. Use the Attribute Web on page 8 of this guide to characterize Beowulf. Analyze the characteristics that make him an ideal king, and discuss any flaws in his character. *(Feelings: confidence, pride, compassion; Demographics: son of Ecgtheow, nephew of Hrethrel, resident of Geatland [Scandinavia]; Actions: defends the Danes against evil, becomes king and rules the Geats wisely, dies fighting the dragon; Prized Possessions: his sword Naegling, his armor, his golden collar. He lives by the heroic code, e.g., he is courageous, loyal, honest, wise, respectful, and noble. He champions freedom from evil oppression and is willing to sacrifice himself for right. Flaw: Wiglaf alludes to Beowulf's failure to listen to counsel before his battle with the dragon, thus leaving the Geats without his leadership and subjecting them to invasion from other nations.)*
3. Using the Sociogram on page 9 of this guide, place Beowulf's name in the center circle and the names of additional characters in the other circles. Utilize descriptive words or phrases to describe each character and the relationship they have with Beowulf. *(Suggestion—the relationship between Beowulf and Hrothgar, Hygelac, Unferth, and Wiglaf. Beowulf proves his courage and saves the Danes from evil; Hrothgar rewards him and warns him against the dangers of pride and power. Hygelac respects him as a brave warrior and a wise member of his court; Beowulf honors him by supporting Heardred as king and later diligently ruling the Geats. Unferth challenges Beowulf's honor but later acknowledges his courage and gives him his own sword, Hrunting; Beowulf accepts the sword and speaks kindly of Unferth. Wiglaf stays with his king and fulfills his final requests; Beowulf gives Wiglaf his treasured golden collar, implying that he views Wiglaf as the one who has the wisdom to lead the nation.)*
4. Use the Story Map on page 10 of this guide to analyze the poem.
5. Use the Sequence graphic organizer on page 11 of this guide. Place the statement, "The wheel has come full circle" at the top of the chart, and analyze the circle of Beowulf's life. *(Suggestion—[1] Beowulf is raised by his uncle, King Hrethel. [2] He proves his courage and stamina in the swimming match with Breca. [3] He responds to the need to destroy evil in Denmark. [4] He returns to Geatland and becomes a wise, judicious king. [5] He dies fighting evil, i.e., the dragon. [6] His body is burned on a funeral pyre, and the Geat warriors build a barrow to memorialize him.)*
6. Analyze the interweaving of Christianity and paganism in the poem. *(References to Christianity may include Hrothgar's attributing Beowulf's coming to Denmark to Almighty God, his thanksgiving for Beowulf's successful venture in ridding the country of evil, and his warning to Beowulf to remember that God rules all things. Hygelac thanks God for Beowulf's safe return. Beowulf attributes his successful campaigns against evil to God's providence and repeatedly gives thanks to God for His help. Paganism is referenced by the numerous allusions to fate, e.g., Beowulf says that fate will decide the winner in his battles with evil.*

All rights reserved

7. Examine the importance of minor characters in the poem. Note especially the portrayal of women in the Anglo-Saxon culture. *(Suggestions—Unferth, who depicts jealousy and who offers his own sword to Beowulf because he is not man enough to use it himself and Wiglaf, who portrays heroic characteristics of a young Beowulf. Wealhtheow and Hygd both represent gracious, faithful queens who are loyal to their husbands and solicitous of the needs of the king's thanes. The references to women as peace-pledges reflect the lack of respect and right of choice many Anglo-Saxon women experienced.)*
8. Analyze examples of symbolism in the poem, e.g., monsters, darkness/light, gold. *(Monsters: the epitome of evil and its invasion into the Dane and Geat civilization, wreaking havoc and grief. Darkness/light: forces of evil and good; Grendel retreats to die in the lake, i.e., hell; Grendel and his mother can only attack at night; Beowulf defeats Grendel's mother in the darkness of the haunted lake, and the place is immediately illuminated. Light in the mead-hall reflects joy and honor, but evil lurks in the dark. Gold: honor, e.g., Beowulf's gifts from Hrothgar; temptation, e.g., the theft of the goblet from the dragon's lair; covetousness, e.g., the dragon's greedy guarding of his hoard.)*
9. Compare and contrast the three battles that Beowulf fights. *(Comparison: All are against superhuman monsters who represent evil; the antagonists are impervious to most human weapons; Beowulf goes into each battle alone; the safety of a nation is at stake. Contrast: Beowulf fights Grendel on his human territory, he fights Grendel's mother on her supernatural territory, and he fights the dragon on the dragon's territory. He fights Grendel without weapons but arms himself for the other two battles. He kills the first two antagonists by himself, but Wiglaf assists him in killing the dragon. He survives the first two battles but dies in the third.)*
10. Examine tenets of the heroic code and the characters in the poem who do or do not adhere to that code. *(Tenets: loyalty, perseverance, integrity, honor, nobility, courage. Beowulf, Hrethel, Hrothgar, Hygelac, and Wiglaf adhere to the code; Unferth abides by portions of the code; the three antagonists have no allegiance to any code of honor.)*
11. Examine the poet's rationale for inserting passages that recapitulate prior events. *(Note that these passages are used to insert a moral lesson, e.g., Heremod's tale, to reveal the devastation of vengeance, i.e., the story of Hildeburh, to fill in the gaps in the story of Beowulf's life.)*

All rights reserved

© Novel Units, Inc.

Post–reading Extension Activities

Note to Teachers: For Writing Assignment #1, have available copies of the Venn Diagram on page 12 of this guide. For Final Assessment #5, place all vocabulary words on slips of paper in a box.

Writing

1. Using the Venn Diagram on page 12 of this guide, compare and contrast Beowulf with another epic hero with whom you are familiar, e.g. Odysseus, or a modern-day hero. Write 2–4 pages, using the information from your diagram.
2. Write a poem of at least 24 lines about someone you know who exemplifies the same characteristics as Beowulf. Use alliteration and caesura in your poem.
3. Write a diamente poem contrasting darkness and light as they are symbolized in the novel. Pattern—Line 1: one word (noun, the title); Line 2: two words (adjectives describing line 1); Line 3: three words ("ing" or "ed" words that relate to line 1); Line 4: four nouns (first two relate to line 1; second two relate to line 7); Line 5: three words ("ing" or "ed" words that relate to line 7); Line 6: two words (adjectives describing line 7); Line 7: one word (noun that is the opposite of line 1). Place on paper in the shape of a diamond.
4. Write a poem about Wiglaf's ascension to the Geat throne.
5. Write ten kennings for people, events, or things in your world.

Art

6. Design a coat-of-arms for Beowulf.
7. Sketch your impression of each of the three antagonists in the poem.
8. Create a collage depicting one of the themes in the poem.
9. Prepare a montage of pictures showing different types of armor used by the Anglo-Saxons.

Research

10. Research and write a 3–5 page paper about the rise of Christianity among the Anglo-Saxons. Cite your references. You can find information and a bibliography at **http://members.tripod.com/~mr_sedivy/engrise5.html.** (Note: This Web site was active at the printing of this guide.)

Music

11. Write and perform a dirge Hildeburh might have sung at the funeral pyre of her son and her brother. (p. 77)
12. Select and play for the class appropriate music for Beowulf's final battle and his death.

All rights reserved

Assessment for *Beowulf*

Assessment is an ongoing process. The following ten items can be completed during the novel study. Once finished, the student and teacher will check the work. Points may be added to indicate the level of understanding.

Name ______________________________ Date ______________

Student	Teacher	
______	______	1. Write three review questions about the poem. Participate in an oral review.
______	______	2. Correct all quizzes over the poem.
______	______	3. Write a riddle about one of the characters in the poem. Exchange with a partner and identify the characters.
______	______	4. Display or perform your extension project on the assigned day.
______	______	5. Draw one vocabulary word from the "vocabulary box." Participate in a game of charades as a vocabulary review by preparing a charade for the class.
______	______	6. Compare your list of kennings with other students in a small group.
______	______	7. Working in small groups, compare your completed character charts, comprehension activities, and story map.
______	______	8. Write a precis of the poem.
______	______	9. Compare your completed vocabulary activities with a partner.
______	______	10. Identify your favorite character (excluding Beowulf), and explain your choice to the class.

All rights reserved

© Novel Units, Inc.

Glossary

Lines 1–319, pp. 3–23

1. foundling (3): a child found deserted
2. torques (7): necklaces of twisted metal
3. anathema (9): a person or thing that has been cursed or consigned to damnation
4. wassail (11): a drinking party; revelry
5. parley (13): to discuss terms, especially with an enemy
6. rabid (13): unreasonably furious; raging
7. thane (15): a man who held land for the king and gave military service in return
8. interlopers (19): those who thrust themselves into the affairs of others
9. mongering (21): causing; trafficking

Lines 320–661, pp. 23–45

1. formidable (27): hard to overcome; to be dreaded
2. lament (31): sorrow and mourn for
3. brook (35): endure; tolerate
4. pinioned (39): bound the arms of
5. mizzle (41): drizzle in fine drops

Lines 662–1007, pp. 45–67

1. mettle (45): courage; to be ready and anxious to do one's best
2. bourne (47): realm; domain
3. bane (49): ruin; harm; curse
4. baleful (49): very evil or harmful
5. canny (49): shrewd and cautious
6. ignominious (57): shameful; disgraceful; contemptible

Lines 1007–1250, pp. 67–89

1. carnage (69): slaughter of a great number of people; massacre
2. coffer (69): container used to hold money or other valuables
3. bereft (71): bereaved; deprived
4. keens (77): wailing laments for the dead
5. boons (83): benefits; blessings; favors

Lines 1251–1491, pp. 89–103

1. sallied (89): rushed forth boldly
2. depredations (93): acts of plundering; robberies by force
3. mere (95): lake or pond
4. hart (95): male deer
5. scud (97): run or move swiftly
6. bulwark (97): defense; protection
7. screes (99): sloping masses of rocky fragments
8. tempered (101): seasoned

Lines 1492–1887, pp. 103–129

1. sage (111): showing wisdom or good judgment; able to give good advice
2. fettle (113): condition or state of readiness for action
3. tender (115): offer in payment
4. damascened (115): gilded, etched, or embossed on steel
5. venerable (115): worthy of reverence; deserving respect; esteemed
6. pariah (119): despised person; outcast

All rights reserved

7. felicity (119): great happiness; bliss
8. overweening (119): thinking too much of oneself; conceited
9. alacrity (125): brisk, eager actions; liveliness
10. gannet (127): large fish-eating sea bird
11. whorled (127): circled with leaves or flowers
12. peerless (129): without any equal; matchless

Lines 1888–2199, pp. 129–149

1. offing (131): distant part of the sea as seen from the shore
2. ensconced (131): settled safely; hidden
3. maw (141): gullet; stomach
4. accoutrement (143): clothing or equipment
5. scion (147): descendant; heir

Lines 2200–2537, pp. 149–171

1. barrow (151): a mound of earth or stones over an ancient grave or pit
2. trove (151): treasure
3. pillage (155): seizing good by force; plunder
4. harrower (155): one who hurts or brings harm
5. gloaming (157): twilight; evening; dusk
6. linden (159): soft, white wood
7. prodigious (161): wonderful; immense; out of the ordinary
8. reconnoitre (163): survey to gain information about the enemy's position and strength
9. wean (165): very young child
10. redress (165): payment; remedy
11. quarter (167): mercy
12. mercenary (169): a person who works solely for monetary gain

Lines 2538–2820, pp. 171–191

1. foiled (175): prevented from succeeding
2. suppurating (183): discharging pus; festering
3. rampart (183): wide band of earth; embankment
4. fomented (185): evoked; promoted
5. filigree (187): delicate, lace-like ornamental wirework of gold or silver
6. pyre (189): pile of wood for burning a dead body as a funeral rite

Lines 2821–3182, pp. 191–213

1. disdainfully (193): proudly; scornfully
2. wake (197): an all-night vigil beside the body of a dead person
3. rout (197): disorderly retreat of a defeated army
4. swathe (199): wrappings; bandages
5. graith (201): equipment; possessions
6. gainsaying (201): denying; disputing
7. dirges (213): funeral songs

All rights reserved

© Novel Units, Inc.

MW01630524
ZÜLAL AYTÜRE-SCHEELE
PAPERFOLDING FUN
ORIGAMI
IN COLOR
GALLERY BOOKS
An Imprint of W.H. Smith Publishers Inc.
112 Madison Avenue
New York City 10016

C ▾ O ▴ N ▾ T ▴ E ▾ N ▴ T ▾ S

First published by Octopus Books Ltd.

This edition published in 1986 by Gallery Books
An imprint of W.H. Smith Publishers Inc.
112 Madison Avenue, New York, New York 10016

© 1986 Falken-Verlag GmbH Niedernhausen/Ts.
West Germany
© 1986 English translation Ridgmount Books Ltd.

Translated by Linda Sonntag

Produced by Mandarin Offset
22a Westlands Road
Quarry Bay Hong Kong

Reprinted 1987, 1988, 1989

ISBN 08317 6673 5

Printed and bound in Hong Kong

FOREWORD

Origami is the Japanese art of paper-folding. It was first practised almost a thousand years ago at the Imperial Court, where it was considered an amusing and elegant way of passing the time. Over the centuries the skill was passed down to the ordinary people, who took it up with enthusiasm and made it into a folk art. Today in Japan the art of paper-folding is as widely practised by children, parents and grandparents as it was centuries ago. And for a number of years now origami has been immensely popular here in the West too. This book will enable you to join the many thousands of people who have already discovered the enjoyment this inexpensive hobby provides.

Eyecatching models – animals, masks, flowers and decorations – are made by simply folding coloured paper. Origami demands concentration, stimulates the imagination and develops dexterity of the fingertips. Apart from that, it's great fun to see a square of paper transformed with a few folds into a pretty flower or a lifelike animal.

Origami can also be put to practical use. You can use the models to make an attractive mobile for a child's bedroom, or you can present someone with a magnificent bunch of flowers on their birthday. You can make masks for carnivals or parties. In this book there are 36 different models to make, based on seven basic shapes.

Here's wishing you a lot of fun in discovering origami.

Zülal Aytüra-Scheele

ORIGAMI PAPER

Japanese shops offer a huge selection of different coloured origami papers. They can be patterned or plain – or plain on one side and patterned on the other. There are large sheets that can be cut down to the size you require, and smaller sheets designed to be worked with straight away. The paper comes in various strengths and qualities. To get genuine Japanese origami paper you don't have to go as far as Japan. It is now available in many stationery shops in this country.

But you can make the models out of lots of different kinds of paper, including good quality gift wrap. When buying paper for origami, you need to make sure that it will fold well and hold a good crease.

It shouldn't tear, stretch or bend when you fold it, so it needs to be both firm and thin.

Buying your paper, choosing patterns and colours to suit the models you are going to make, is a pleasure in itself. Once you have a little experience in paper-folding, you will find that selecting the paper is as much a part of the art of origami as folding it.

Use whatever paper you like to make the models in this book. Special papers are specified where they are required.

GOLDEN RULES

To start off with, here are a few rules to follow to make paper-folding easier.

1 Always work on a smooth flat surface.
2 Measure your paper exactly and cut it accurately and cleanly.
3 Make your folds carefully. Run your thumbnail along the crease each time you make a fold to make it sharp.
4 Begin by folding the basic shape required for the model you have chosen. You will find it more convenient to work through the book from beginning to end, as some models are based partially on previous ones.
5 The instruction steps should be followed in sequence. They won't make sense if read in isolation.
6 If one of your folds – or even a whole model – goes wrong, don't lose heart. Go through all the steps carefully one by one, checking that you have followed the instructions properly and not missed a vital word or overlooked an arrow or dotted line.

FOLDING PRACTICE

Folding paper is not difficult, but it does get easier with practice. Get your fingers on the right track with the exercise below. Remember, the neater your folds, the better all your models will look.

Please don't lose heart if you are not successful straight away with this exercise. It is essential to persevere until you master the knack; this should take no more than 10–15 minutes. Once you have got the hang of these key paper-folding techniques you will be ready to tackle with confidence the wide variety of paper models featured on the pages that follow.

1 Start with a square of paper.

2 Fold it in half diagonally towards you. Now fold the lefthand edges in to meet the diagonal crease.

3 Fold the top and bottom halves together, with the white side of the paper inside.

4 Fold the lefthand side up so that the point is vertical. Make a crease and . . .

5 . . . fold it back again. Open up the shape from beneath and . . .

6 . . . fold the lefthand point . . .

7 . . . outwards, to where you made the crease in step 3.

By practising these folds you have already made a simple duck.

8 Firm along the fold. Fold the top point . . .

9 . . . over to the left.

10 Unfold the point again and open it out a little.

11 Fold the point along the crease you have just made . . .

12 . . . over and down . . .

13 . . . to the left.

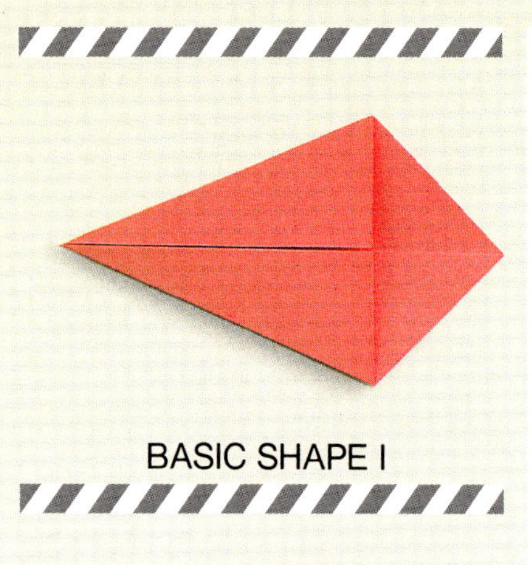

BASIC SHAPE I

1 Start with a square of paper.

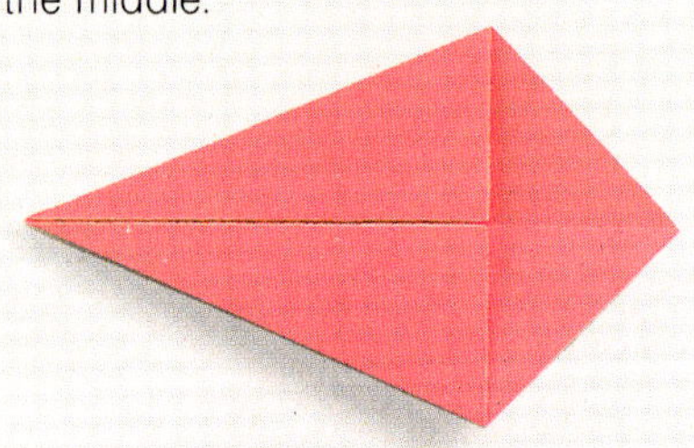

2 Fold it towards you diagonally in the middle.

3 Fold the lefthand edges in to meet the diagonal crease. This is Basic Shape I.

SWAN

1 Begin with Basic Shape I. Fold the top over towards you, leaving the flaps inside.

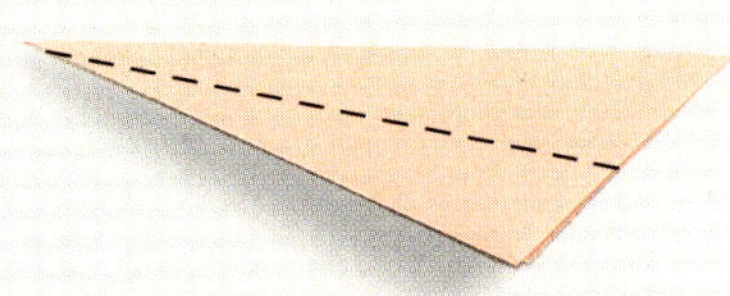

2 Fold the paper up along the dotted line. Repeat on the other side.

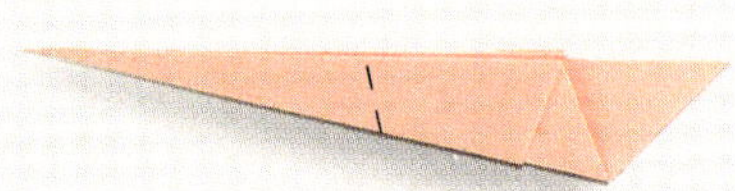

3 Fold the lefthand point up along the dotted line. Make a crease and . . .

4 . . . fold it down again.

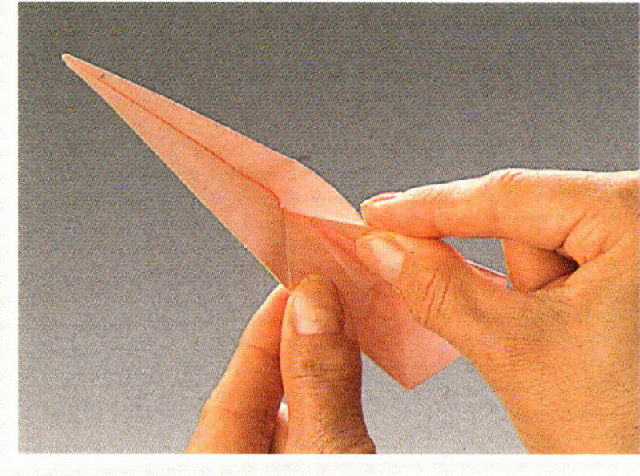

5 Open the shape out from beneath.

6 Along the crease you've just made, fold the left side of the shape . . .

7 . . . upwards. Along the line indicated, fold the point . . .

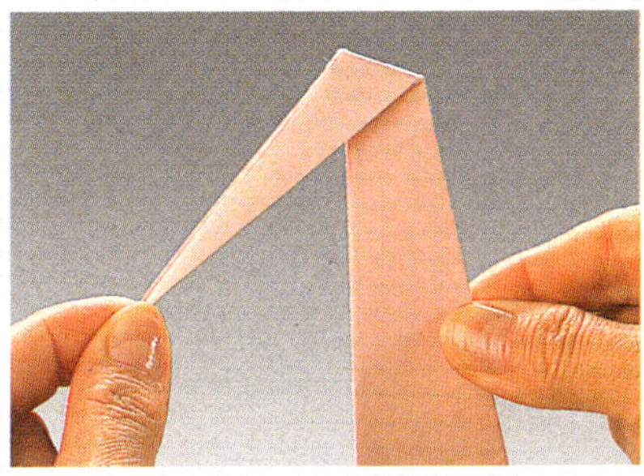

8 . . . down to the left. Make a crease.

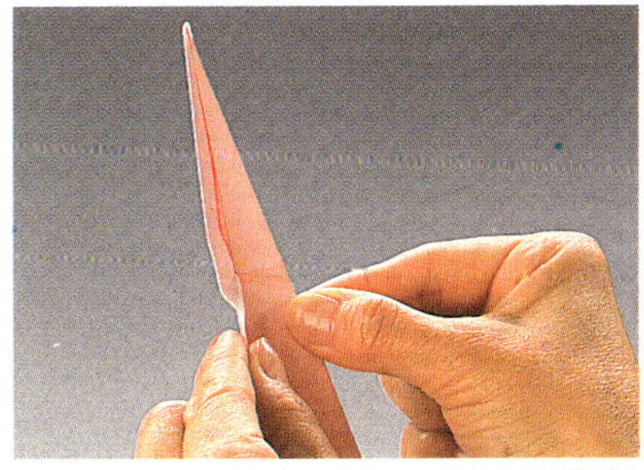

9 Unfold it again, opening out the point.

10 Fold the point over to the left along the crease you have just made.

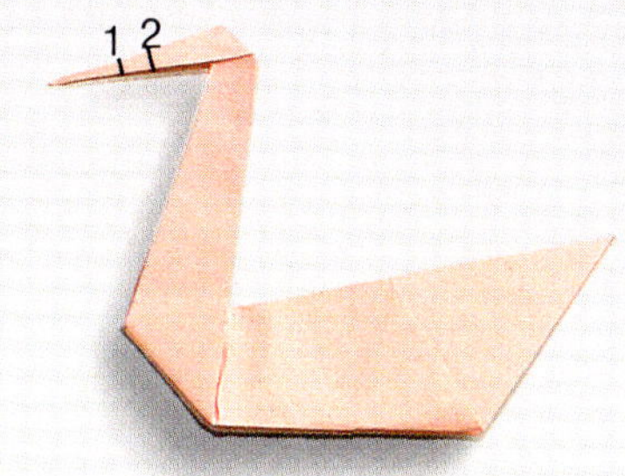

11 On the two lines indicated . . .

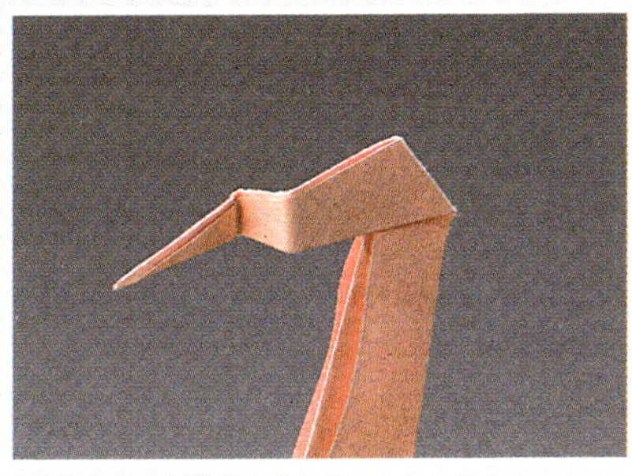

12 . . . make parallel folds.

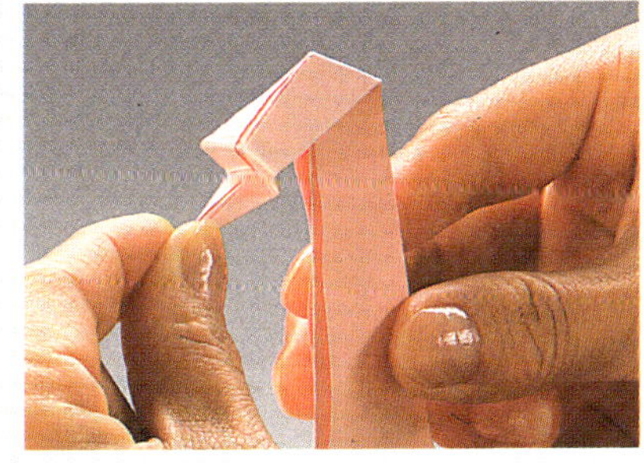

13 Fold the paper inwards on the first crease, and outwards on the second.

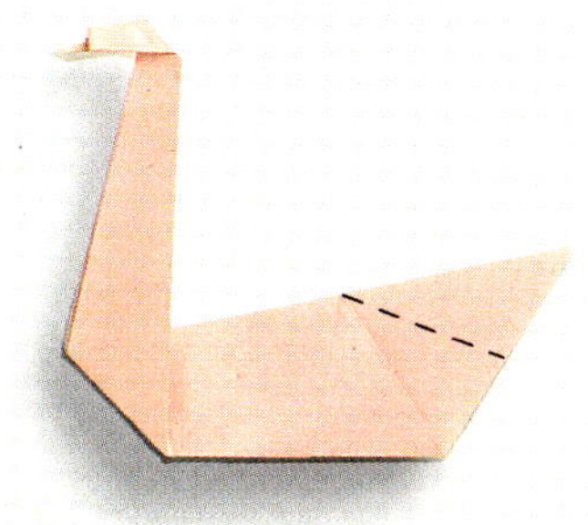

14 On the line indicated . . .

15 . . . fold the tail forwards . . .

16 . . . and inwards along the crease.

17 Pull the point of the tail up, press it in towards the centre and make a fold to hold it there.

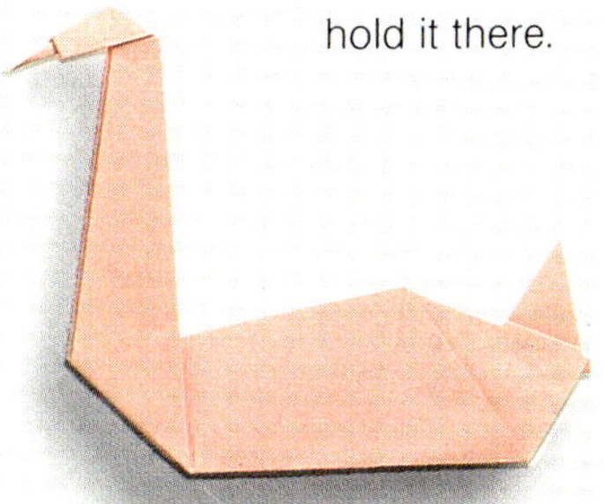

18 The finished swan.

CYGNET

1 Start with Basic Shape I (p.8). Fold the white triangle along the dotted line . . .

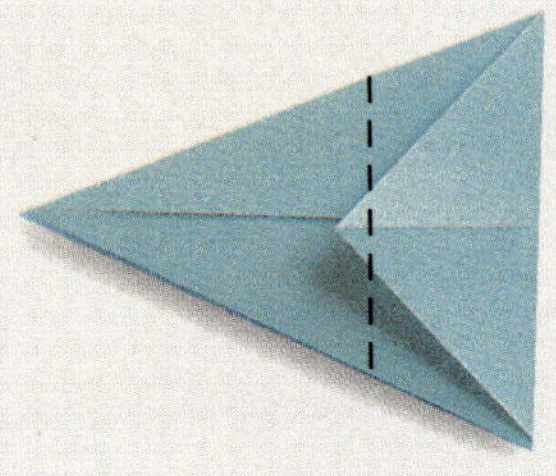

2 . . . in to the left. Fold the left point along the dotted line . . .

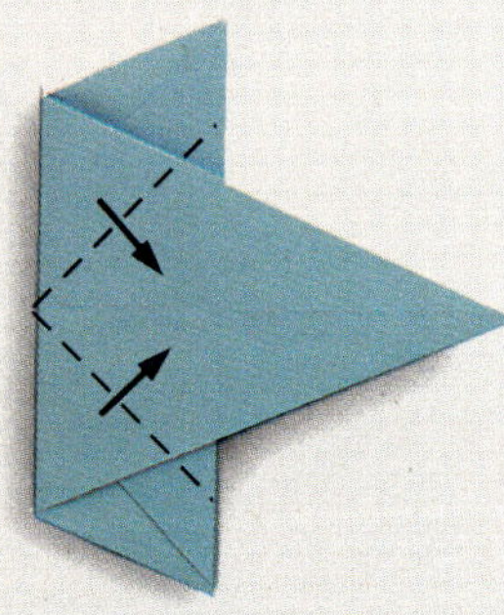

3 . . . in to the right. Fold the lefthand top and bottom sections in along the dotted lines . . .

4 . . . to meet at the horizontal centre fold.

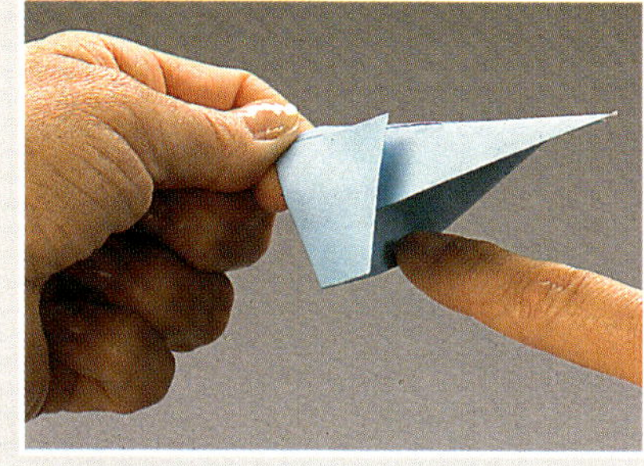

5 Pick up the shape and open it out from underneath.

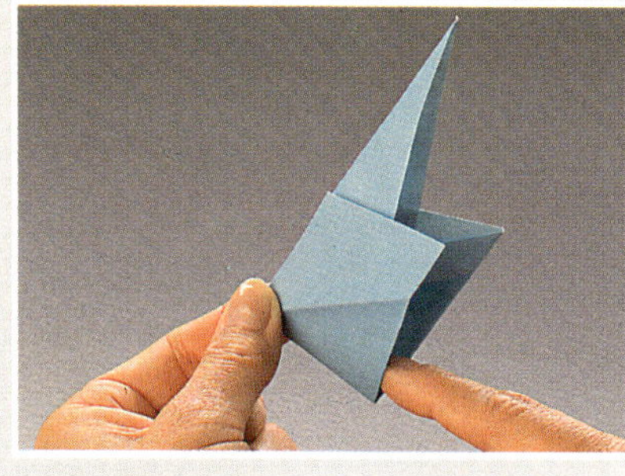

6 Fold the two wings together.

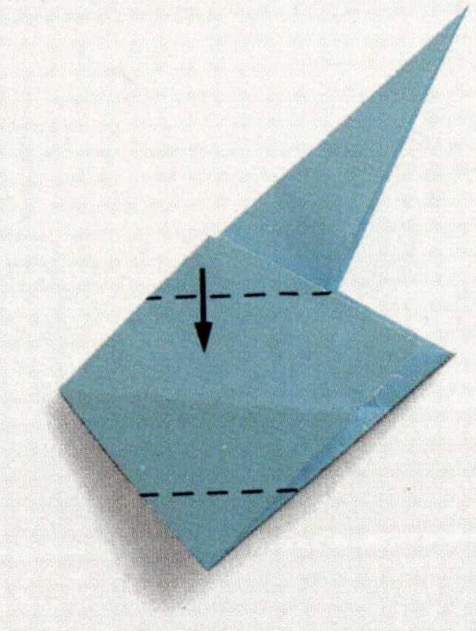

7 Fold the wingtip down on the dotted line. Repeat on the other side. Fold the front bottom point up on the lower dotted line.

8 Make a crease on the dotted line.

9 Open the point out and fold it over to the left along the crease.

10 Open the shape out along the bottom fold and press the small triangle inwards. Fold the head in on the first line . . .

11 . . . and out on the second line. The cygnet is finished.

BABY MONKEY

1 Start with Basic Shape I (p.8). Fold the righthand top and bottom sections in on the dotted lines . . .

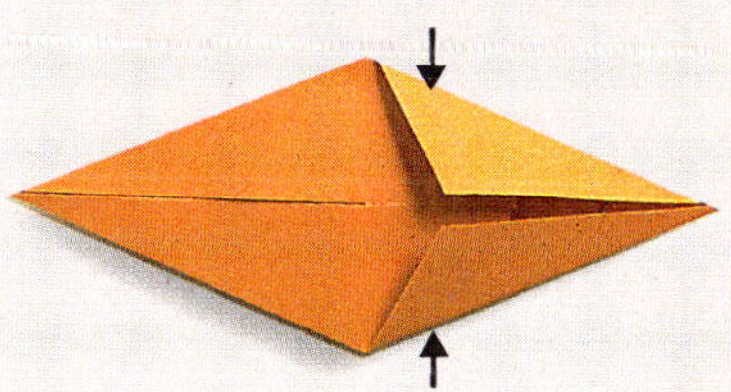

2 . . . to meet at the horizontal centre fold. At the arrows, fold the righthand point . . .

3 . . . in to the left. Fold it back along the dotted line . . .

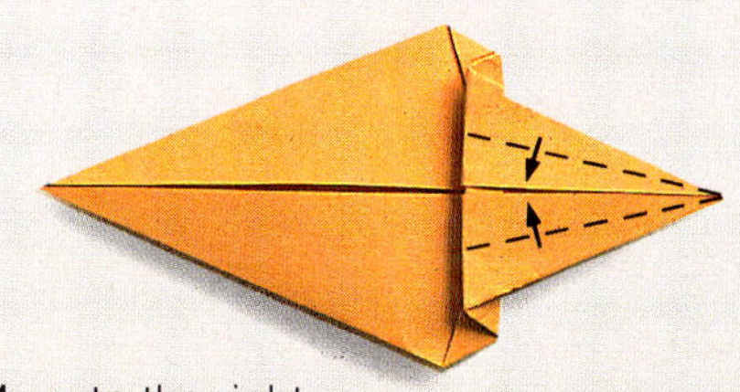

4 . . . to the right.
Working on the righthand triangle . . .

5 . . . fold the bottom section up along the dotted line . . .

6 . . . and fold flat the small triangle that has formed at the left.

7 Repeat on the righthand side.
Fold the top down . . .

8 . . . to meet the bottom. Fold the lefthand point up on the dotted line.

9 Open up the lefthand side of the shape . . .

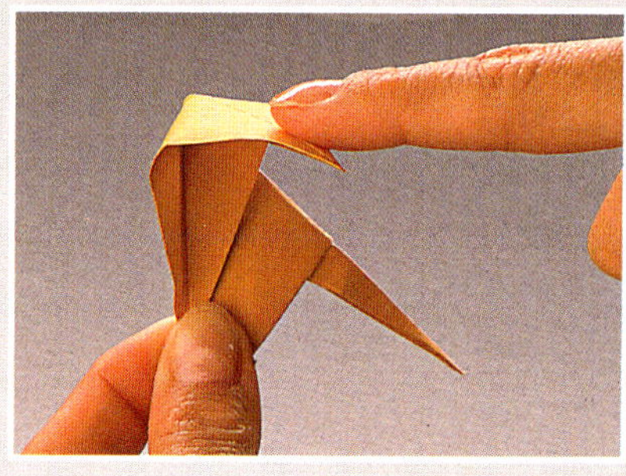

10 . . . and bring the top down, folding it flat.

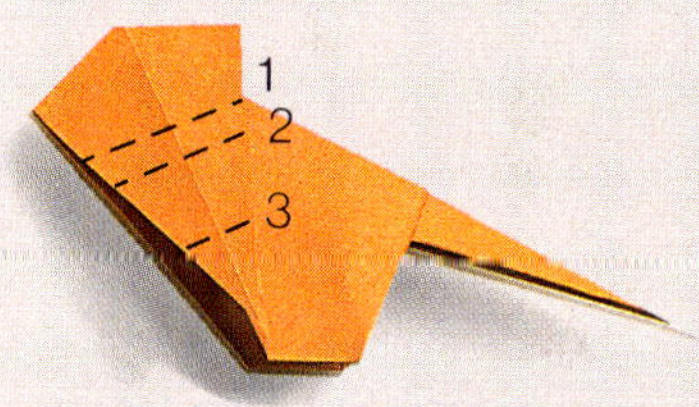

11 Make three parallel folds along the lines indicated. Fold the first in, the second out, and the third in.

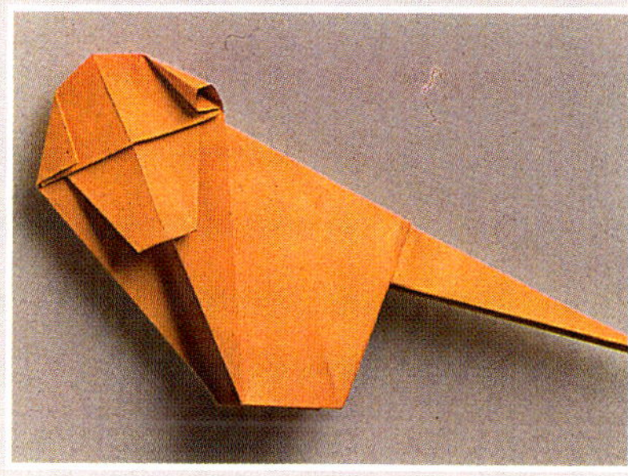

12 Fold the top right and lefthand corners forward and round them out to form ears. The baby monkey is ready.

PEACOCK

THE PAPER

A A small sheet of paper for the body (about 10 × 10 cm)

B A second sheet of paper, four times bigger than the first, for the tail (about 20 × 20 cm)

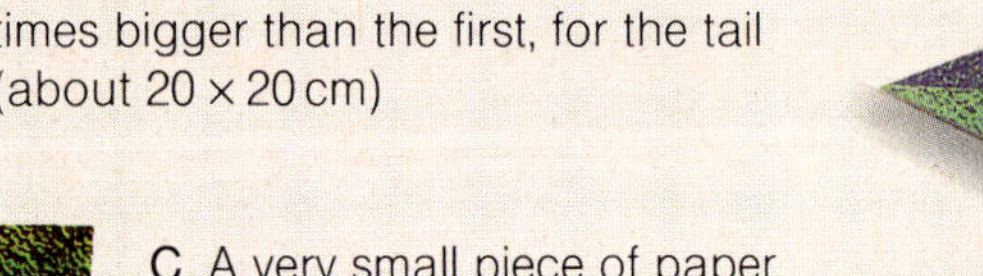

C A very small piece of paper for the crown (about 3 × 3 cm)

THE BODY

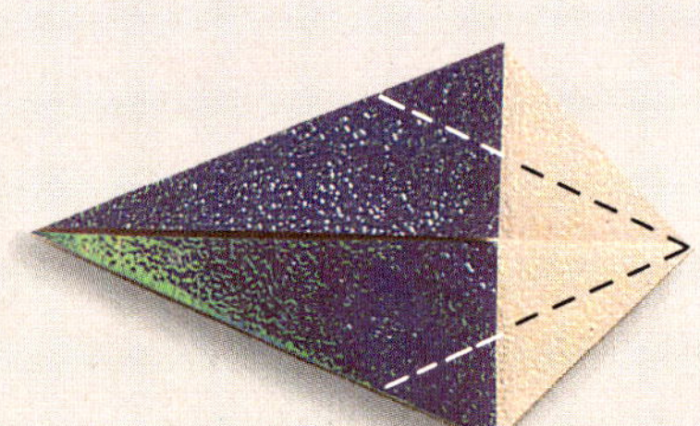

1 Make Basic Shape I (p.8) with paper A. Along the dotted lines fold the righthand top . . .

2 . . . and bottom sections in to meet at the horizontal centre fold. Turn the shape over.

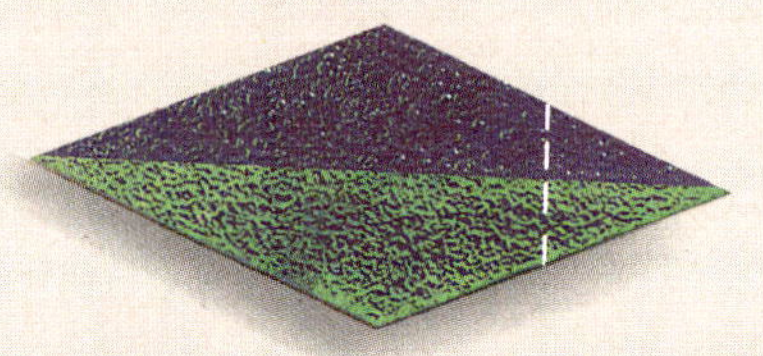

3 Fold the righthand point along the dotted line . . .

4 . . . over to the left. Fold the top half over along the centre fold to meet the bottom half.

5 Fold the lefthand point along the dotted line . . .

6 . . . over and up.

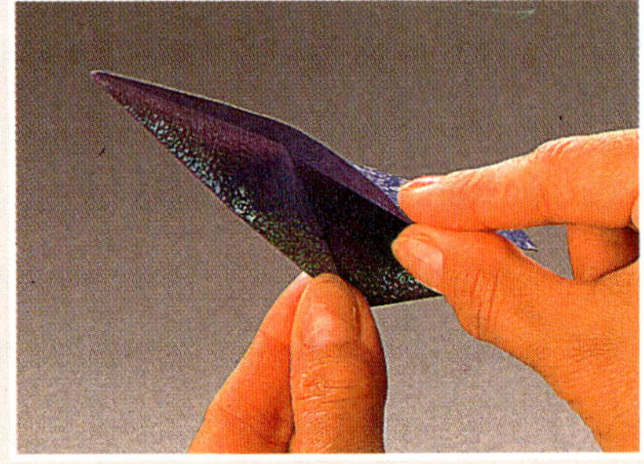

7 Open out point from beneath . . .

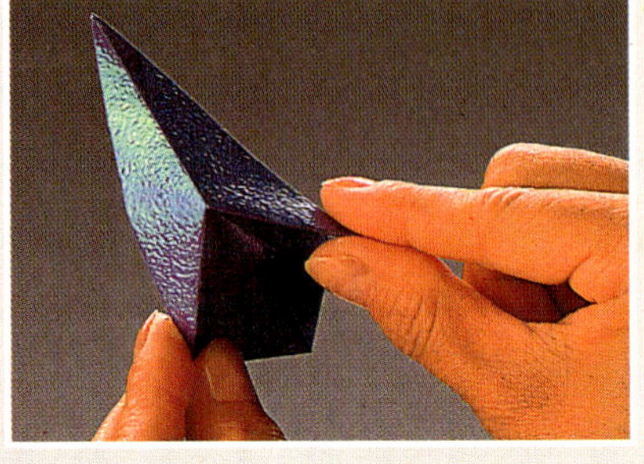

8 . . . and fold it up and out along the crease you have already made.

9 Fold the point over on the line indicated.

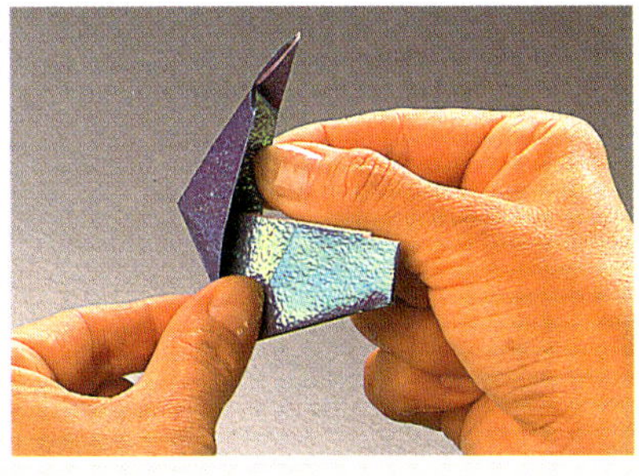

10 Open up the point.

11 Fold the point over to the left on the crease you have just made.

12 Now the body is ready.

THE TAIL

1 Take paper B and fold it in accordion pleats.

2 Fold it in half.

3 Slot the body in place between the two halves of the tail. Stick the centre edges of the tail together with glue.

THE CROWN

1 Take paper C and fold it in accordion pleats.

2 Fold it in half and stick the centre edges together with glue.

3 Stick the crown in place on the peacock's head.

PENGUIN

1 Start with Basic Shape I (p.8). Along the dotted lines . . .

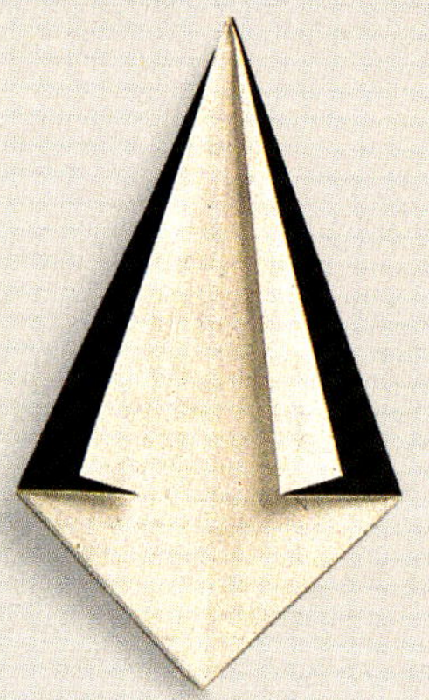

2 . . . fold the right and left wings outwards. Turn the shape over.

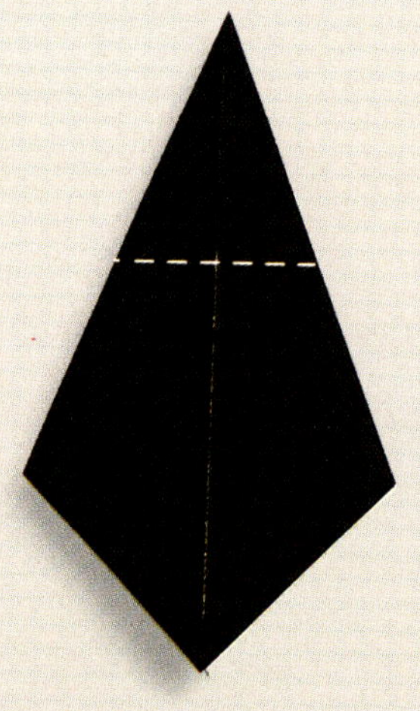

3 Fold the top point down along the dotted line.

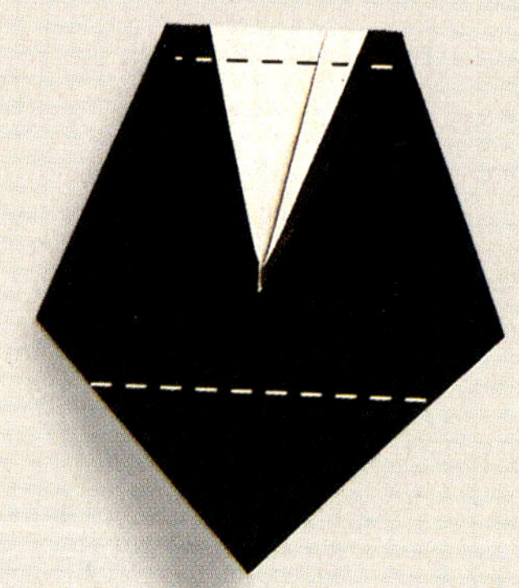

4 Fold the top and bottom points up along the dotted lines.

5 Fold the shape in half along the centre fold.

6 Take the top point . . .

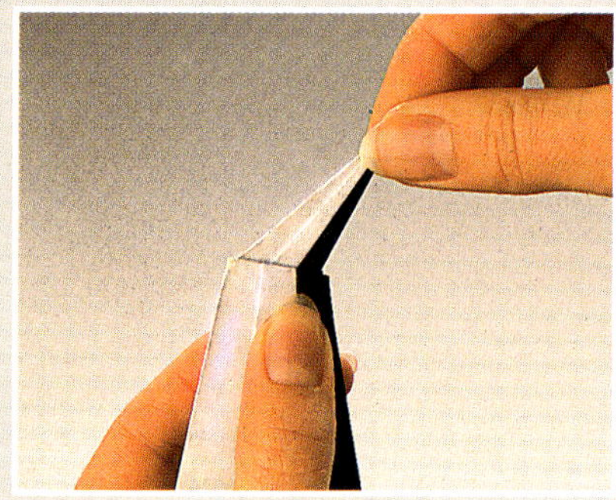

7 . . . and pull it down to the right. Make a fold to hold it there.

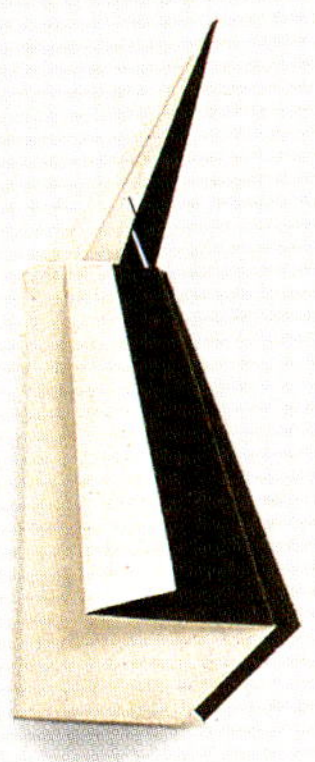

8 Fold the point along the line indicated . . .

9 . . . over to the left.

10 Open out the fold.

11 Fold the point out along the crease you have just made.

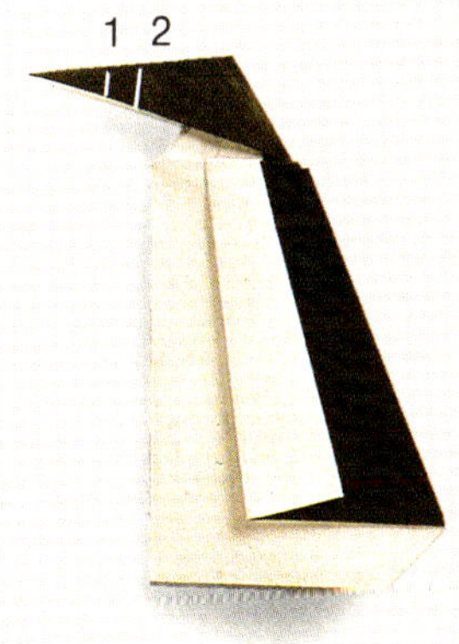

12 Make two parallel folds along the lines indicated.

13 Fold the point to the left along the first line, and to the right along the second.

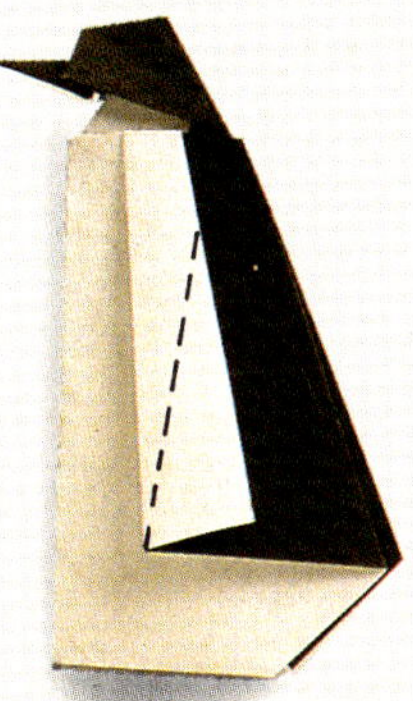

14 Fold the wing along the dotted line to the left. Repeat on the other side.

15 Fold the front righthand section of the figure inwards along the dotted line. Repeat on the other side.

16 The penguin is now finished.

JUNGLE SCENE

ELEPHANT

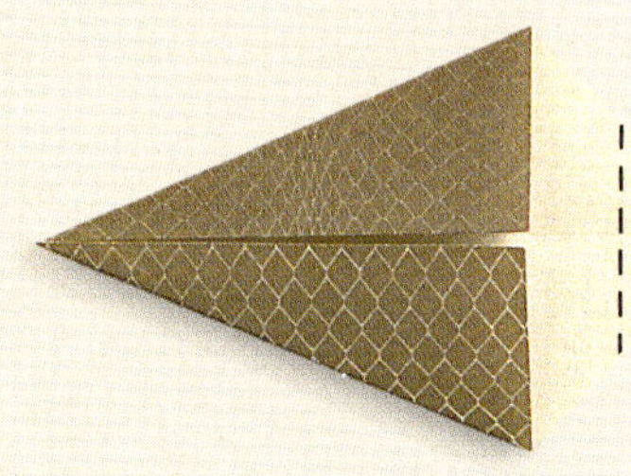

1 Begin with Basic Shape I (p.8). Fold the righthand corner along the dotted line . . .

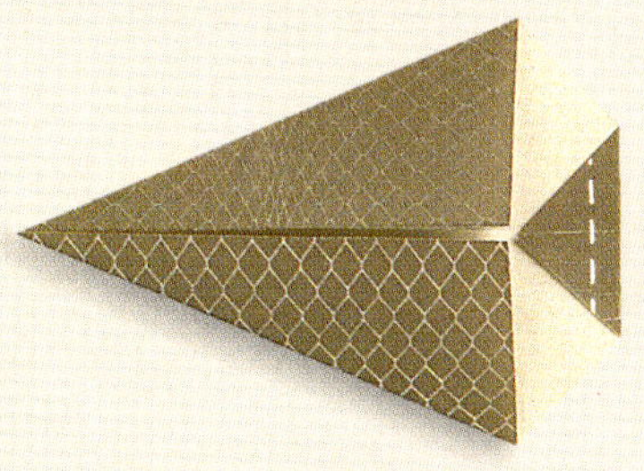

2 . . . to the left. Fold the point along the dotted line . . .

3 . . . back to the right. Turn the shape over.

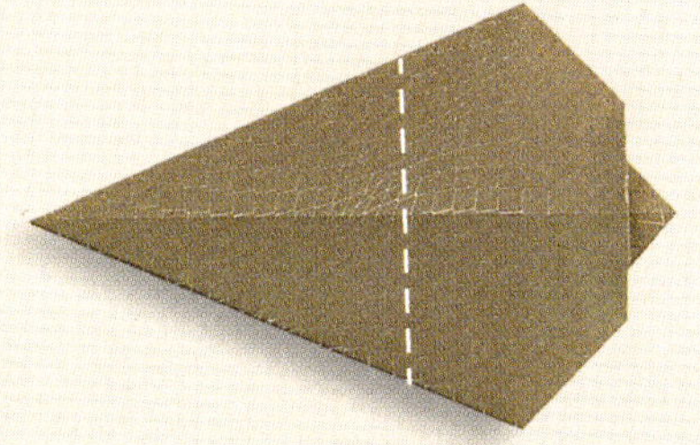

4 Fold the lefthand point along the dotted line to the right.

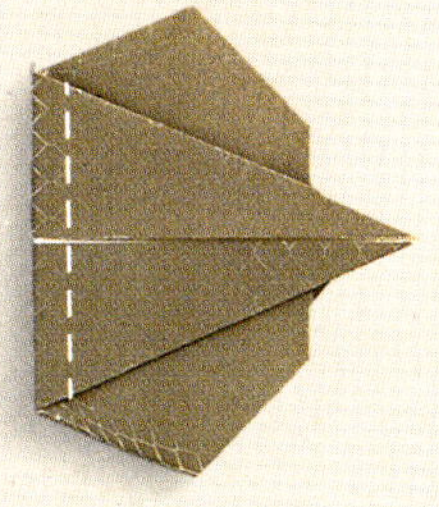

5 Fold the point back along the dotted line . . .

6 . . . to the left. Fold the shape in half along the centre fold.

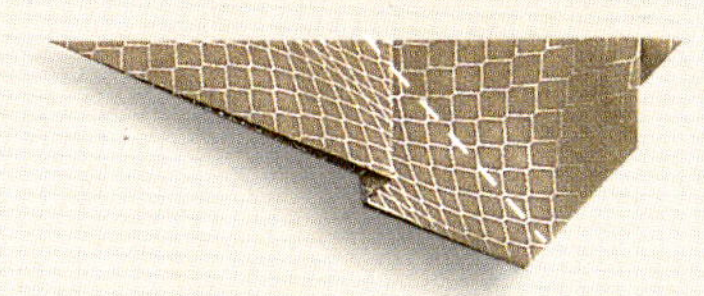

7 Make a crease along the dotted line.

8 Open out the shape from beneath.

9 Fold the paper out along the crease you have already made.

10 Make a crease along the dotted line.

11 Open out the head a little from beneath.

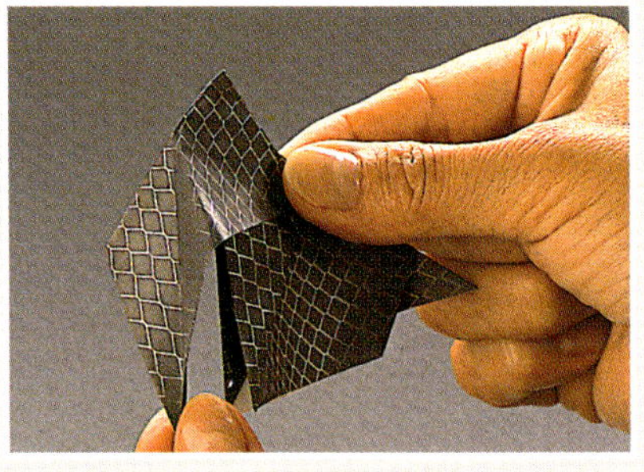

12 Fold the point inwards on the crease you have already made.

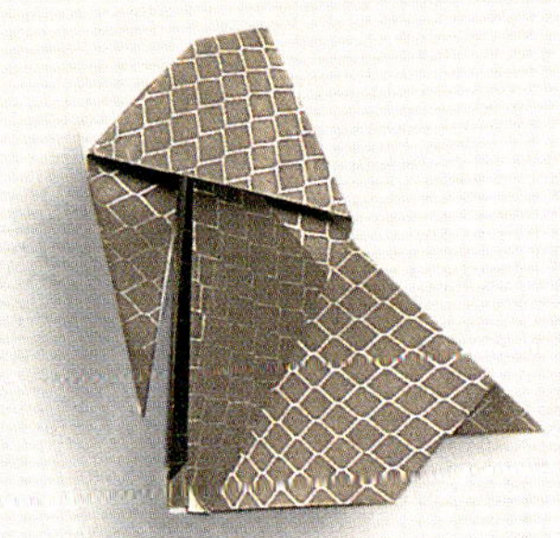

13 Make sharp creases on the lines indicated.

14 Open the paper out and push the resulting small triangle . . .

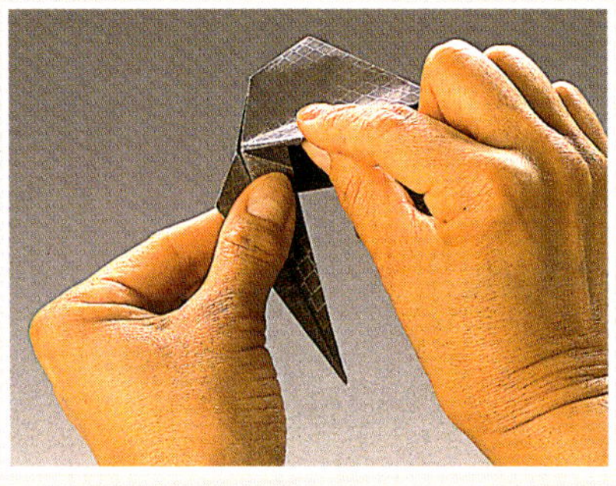

15 . . . in. Repeat on the other side.

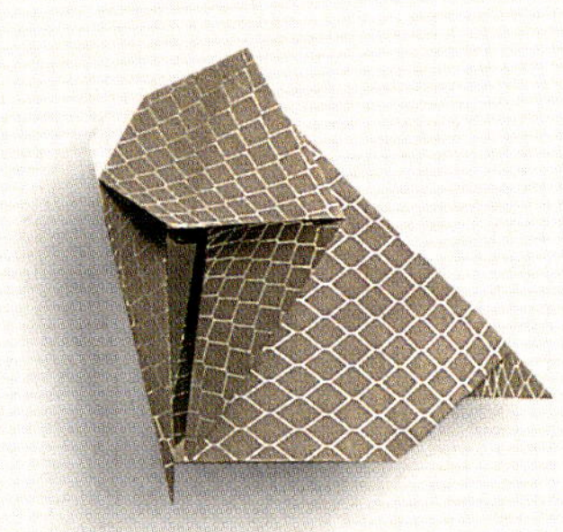

16 Along the dotted line, pull the trunk . . .

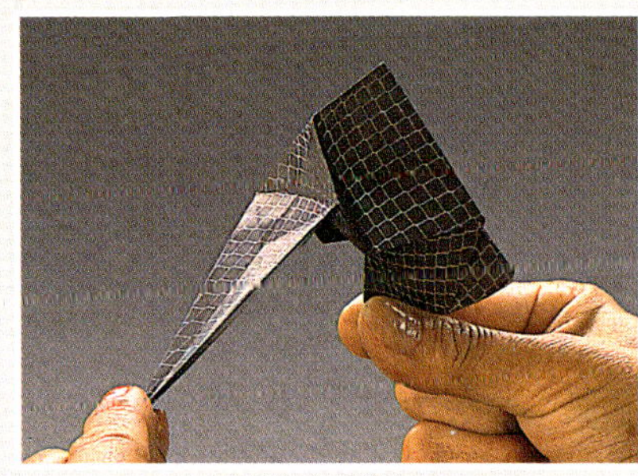

17 . . . out and up.

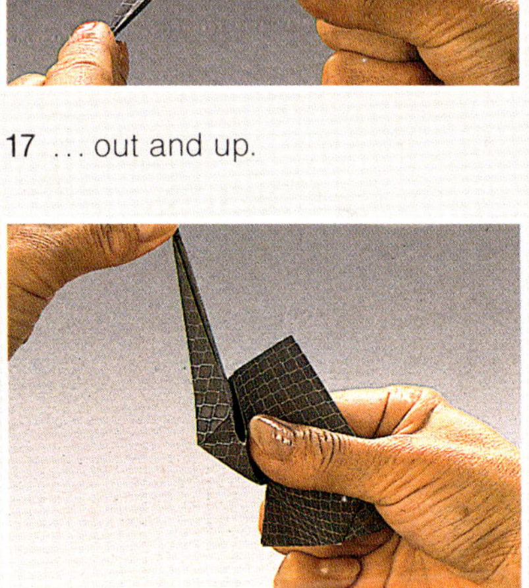

18 Press the trunk flat and make a fold to hold it there.

19 Fold the end of the trunk to the left along the line indicated. Open the point out above the fold . . .

20 . . . and turn it to the left, making a rhomboid shape. Make a fold to hold it there and fold the tip inwards once again.

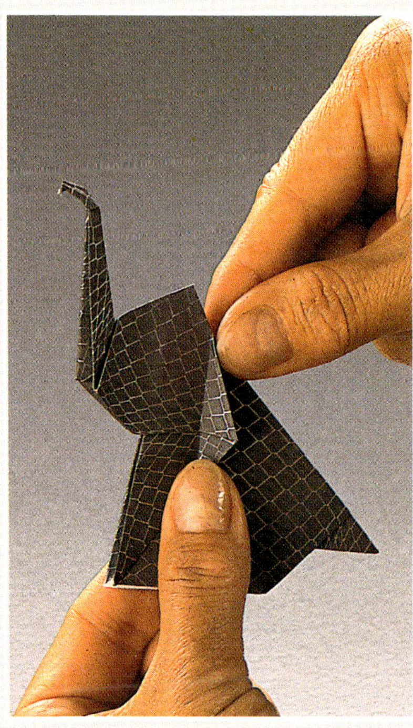

21 Fold both ears forwards, and the elephant is finished.

PIRATE MASK

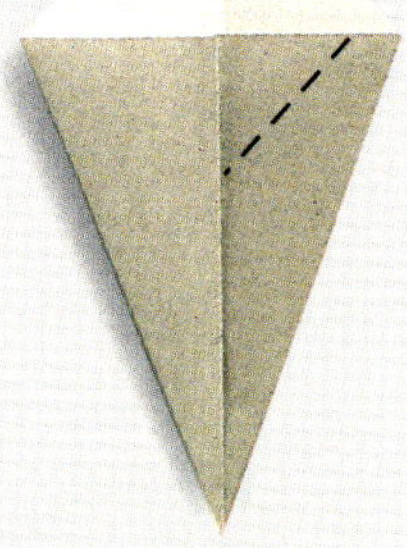

1 Begin with Basic Shape I (p.8). Along the dotted line, fold the inner righthand corner . . .

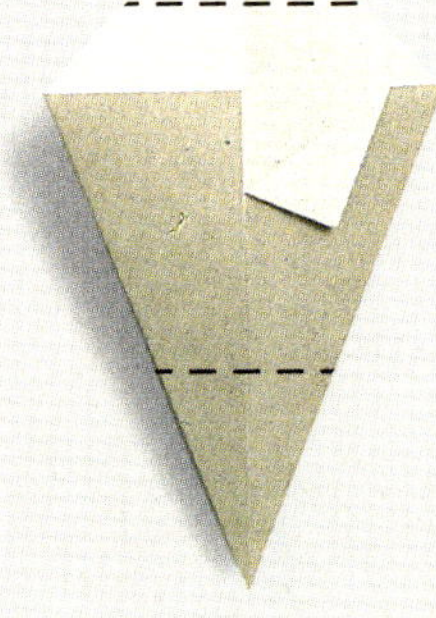

2 . . . down. Fold the upper and lower points towards the centre on the dotted lines.

3 Make two folds along the dotted lines. Pull the triangle out, fold it back inwards on the lower line, and out again on the upper line.

PUPPY

1 Begin with step 10 of the elephant (p.18). Make two parallel folds along the lines indicated.

2 Fold the lefthand point in at the righthand line, and out at the left-hand line.

3 Fold the lefthand point in at the line indicated.

4 The finished puppy.

8 Fold the headscarf along dotted line 2 . . .

9 . . . to give it a knotted effect.

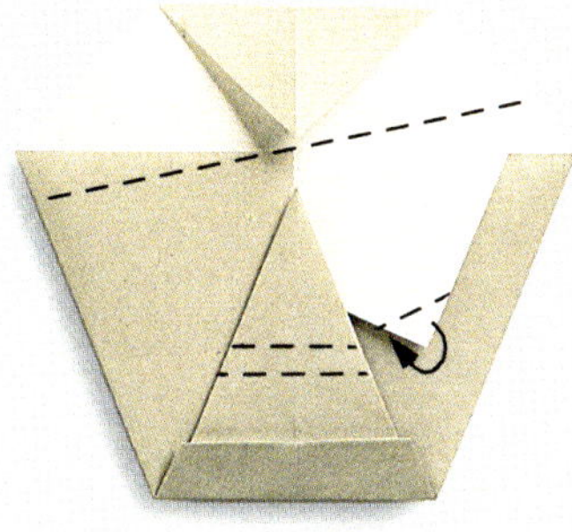

4 Lay the triangle back against the shape. Fold the top down along the dotted line. Fold the tip of the eyepatch back with the arrow. For the nose, make two parallel folds.

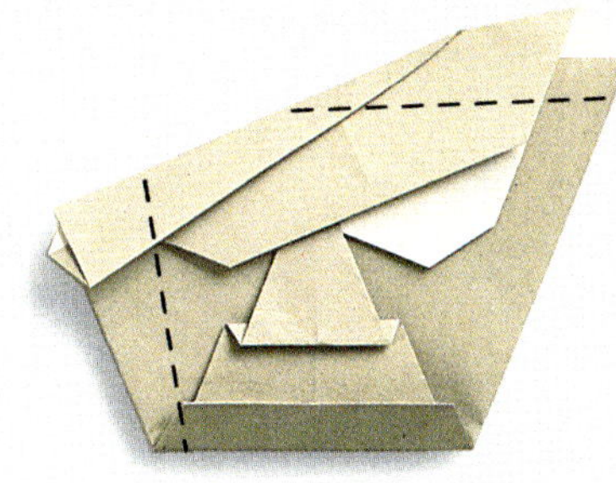

6 Fold the headscarf forwards over the eyepatch. Fold the lefthand side of the figure back along the dotted line.

10 Pull out the nose.

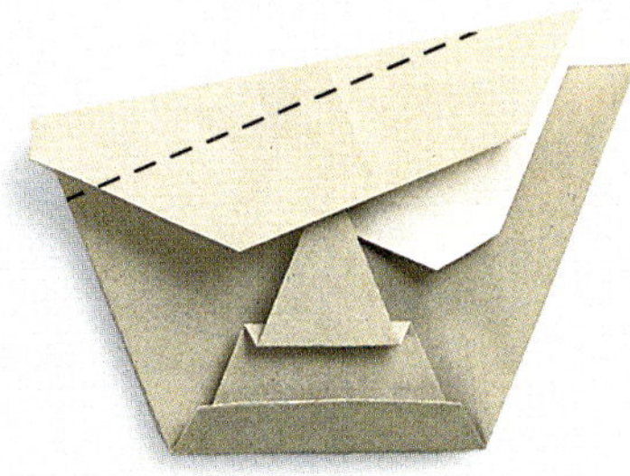

5 Fold the tip of the triangle down and inwards along the upper dotted line, and fold it up and out again along the lower dotted line. Fold the headscarf forwards along the dotted line.

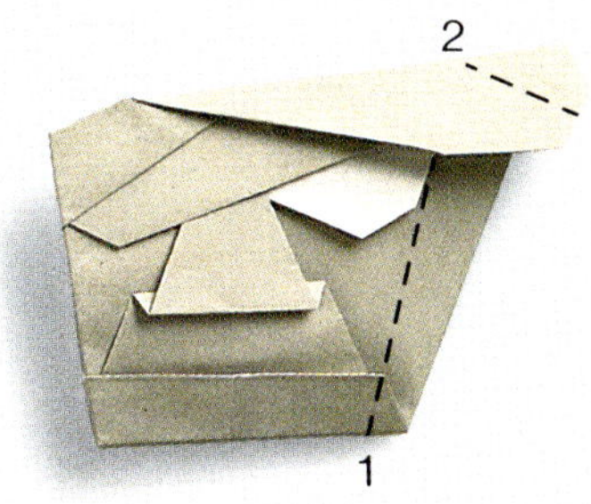

7 Fold the righthand side of the figure back along dotted line 1.

11 Paint the eyepatch black and the headscarf red, and the pirate mask is complete.

DECORATIONS

BASIC SHAPE II

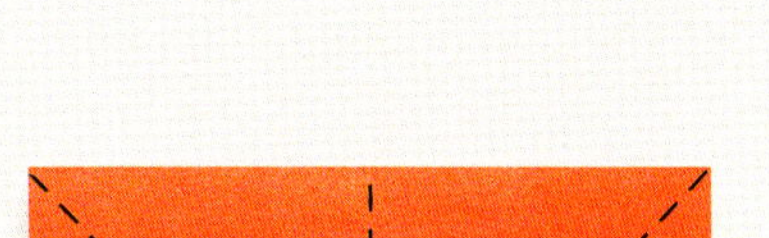

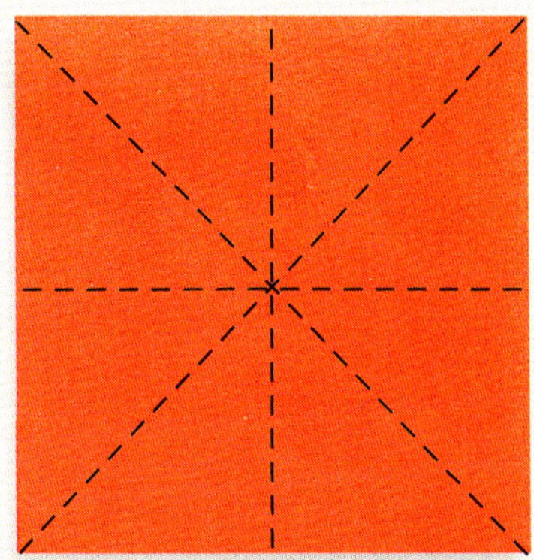

1 Fold a square piece of paper into eight along the dotted lines indicated. Open it out again

2 Fold the right and left sides in together along the vertical centre fold, white side inside.

3 Fold the upper and lower sections in together along the horizontal centre fold. Unfold them.

4 Along the dotted lines, fold the shape first to the right . . .

5 . . . and then to the left.

6 Lift the inner lower corners up and out.

7 Fold up the lower edge of the shape to meet the horizontal centre fold.

8 Turn the shape upside down and repeat steps 6 and 7.

9 This is Basic Shape II.

WINDMILL

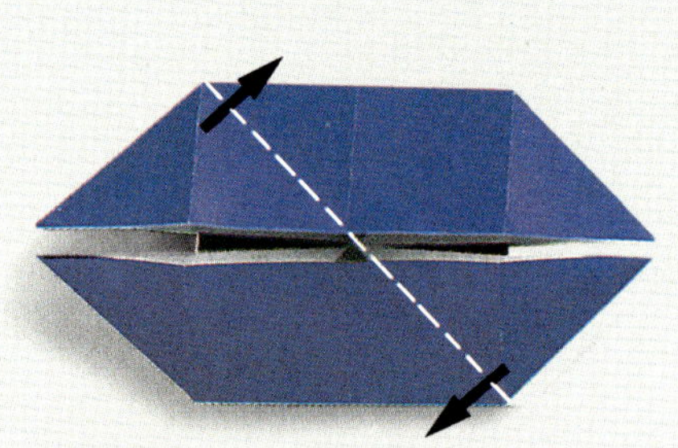

1 Begin with Basic Shape II (p.23). Along the dotted lines . . .

2 . . . fold the lefthand triangle up and the righthand triangle down.

3 The finished windmill.

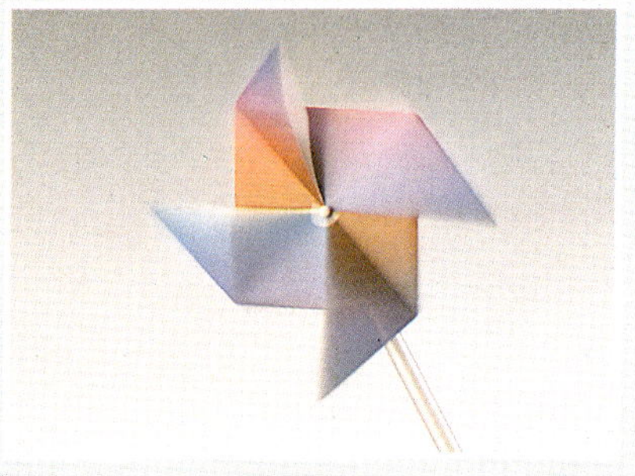

4 You can fix the windmill to a stick with a pin or small nail. Blow, and it will turn.

POMANDER

1 Begin with a windmill.

2 Lift one of the sails vertically upwards.

3 Open it out . . .

4 . . . and press it together with the point inwards. Repeat with the other three sails.

5 Fold the inner two edges of each small square over on the dotted lines to meet at the centre.

6 Lift the righthand fold vertically . . .

7 . . . open it out . . .

8 . . . and press it down flat. Repeat with the lefthand fold. Repeat for each square.

9 Fold the four corners of the shape back along the dotted lines.

10 Stick a round piece of paper in the middle of the flower.

11 Make six flowers and stick them together at the corners to form a ball. The pomander is complete.

ANGEL FISH

You will need a square sheet of paper. If you don't want the mouth of the fish to be white, cut another equal sized square of paper in the colour of your choice and stick the two sheets together, white sides inwards.

1 Fold the paper along the lines indicated. Unfold it again.

2 Fold the top lefthand corner down to the centre point. Turn the shape over.

3 From here, work as for Basic Shape II (p.23). First fold the right and left sides in . . .

4 . . . to meet at the vertical centre fold. Then fold the upper and lower sections in . . .

5 … to meet at the horizontal centre fold.

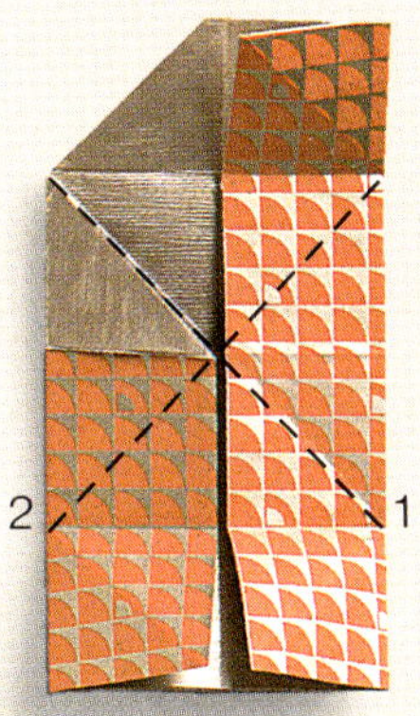

6 Fold them back out again. Fold the lower left side of the shape along dotted line 1 …

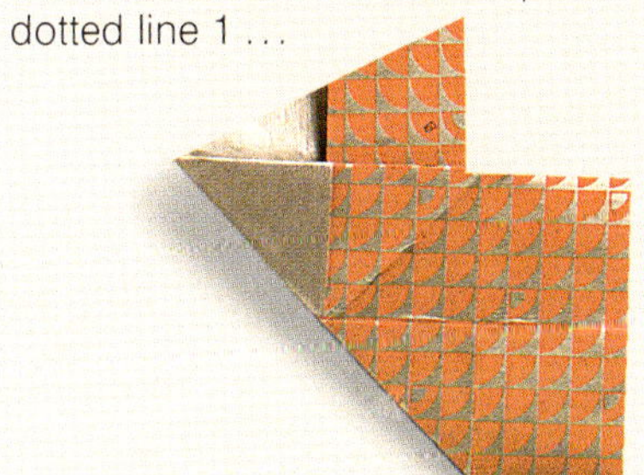

7 … up and over to the right.

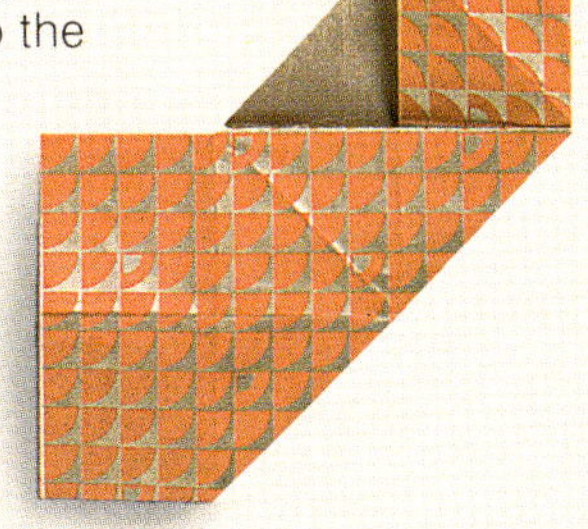

8 Unfold it. Fold the lower right side of the shape along dotted line 2, up and over to the left. Unfold it.

9 Lift the inner bottom corners up and pull them out.

10 Fold up the lower edge of the shape to meet the horizontal centre fold.

11 Pull the top point out and down so that the upper edge of the shape meets the horizontal centre fold.

12 Fold the lower two triangles down on the dotted lines.

13 Fold the lower righthand point up along the dotted line.

14 Turn the shape over …

15 … and the angel fish appears.

BASIC SHAPE III

1 Take a square piece of paper.

2 Fold it on the diagonal with the white side inside.

3 Along the dotted lines, fold the left and righthand ...

4 ... corners down to meet the bottom point.

HAT

1 Begin with Basic Shape III, open points facing downwards.

2 Take the open points and fold them back up to the top. Along the lines indicated ...

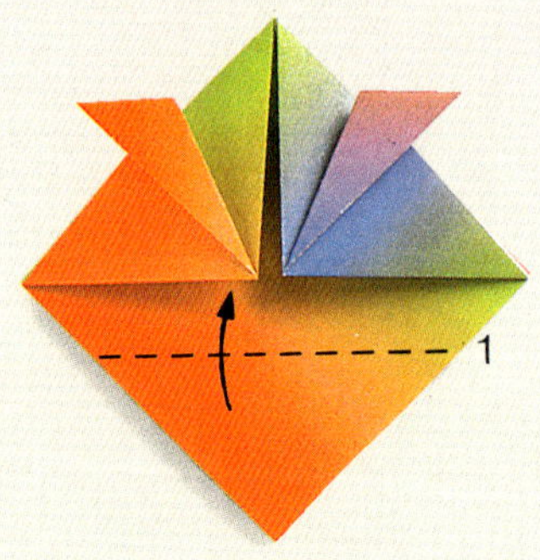

3 ... fold the wings out to the right and left. Along dotted line 1, fold the front point up to the top.

4 Along dotted line 2, fold the paper up again.

5 Fold the remaining lower triangle to the back.

6 The finished hat.

7 Open up the shape.

GOLDFISH

1 Start with the hat.

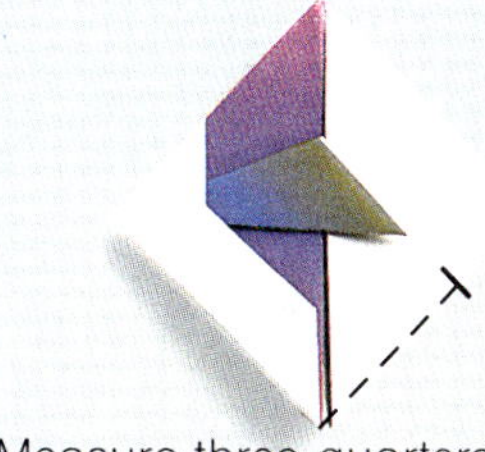

4 Measure three-quarters of the way along the lower righthand side . . .

8 Pull the tail down from the top corner and fold it out.

2 Open it out . . .

5 . . . and cut along the fold to that point.

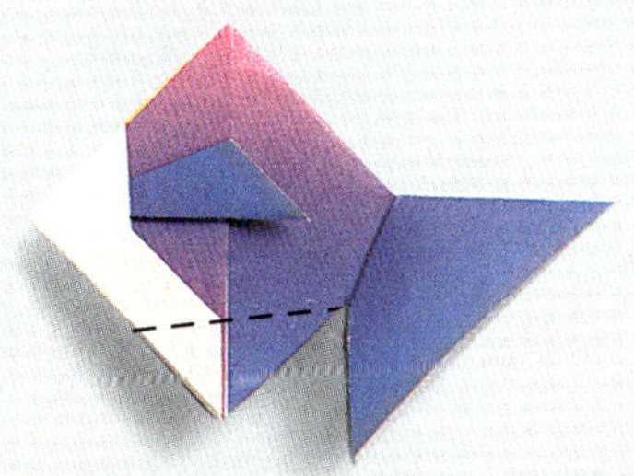

9 Fold the lower edge of this side of the fish in along the dotted line. Repeat with the other side.

3 . . . and fold both the sides together.

6 Make a sharp fold along the line indicated.

10 The finished goldfish.

Variation
You can fold the fin down and paint the mouth or cover it with coloured paper.

BASIC SHAPE IV

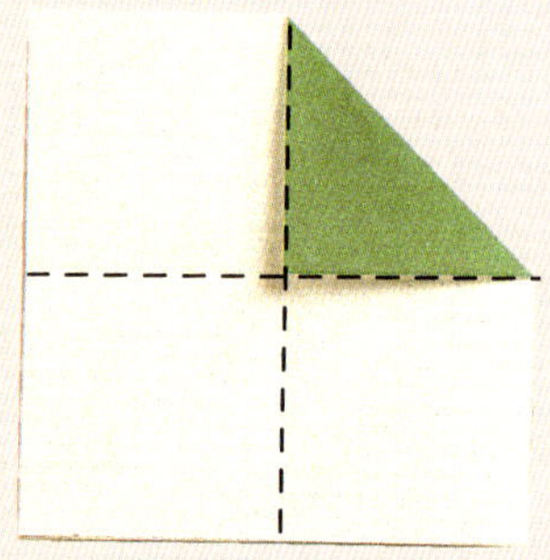

1 Take a square sheet of paper and fold it into four along the dotted lines. Unfold it. Fold each corner ...

2 ... in to the centre.

3 This is Basic Shape IV.

TUG

1 Begin with Basic Shape IV. Turn the shape over.

2 Fold the four corners ...

3 ... in to the centre. Turn the shape over again.

4 Fold the four outer corners ...

5 ... in to the centre. Turn the shape over.

6 Now you have four small squares within one larger one.

7 Open out one of the small squares.

8 Repeat with the square opposite. These are the two funnels.

9 Pull the central corners of the remaining two squares to the outside, bringing the two funnels together.

10 Colour in the rings around the funnels. The tug is now ready to float.

SANTA

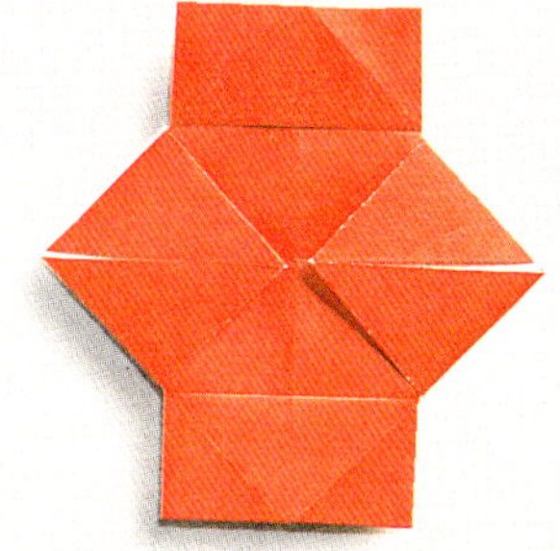

1 Begin with step 8 of the tug (the two funnels are above and below).

2 Open out a third square ...

3 ... and press it flat.

4 Fold the paper in along the dotted lines ...

5 ... to make the arms.

6 The fourth square forms the head. Paint Santa's face, add a beard and trim the coat. He's ready.

TABLE DECORATIONS

PICTURE FRAME

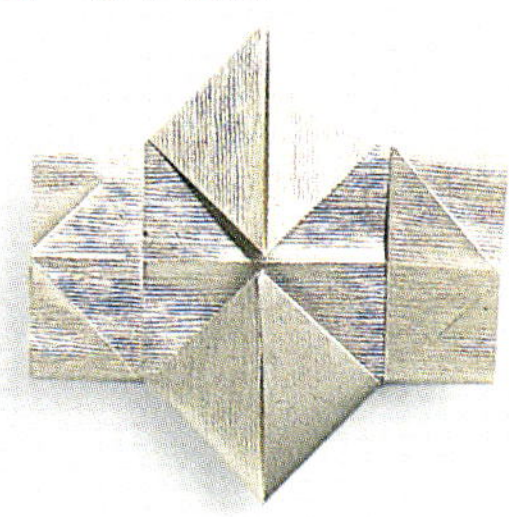

1 Begin with step 8 of the tug (p.31). Open up the two remaining closed squares . . .

2 . . . and press them flat. Turn the shape over.

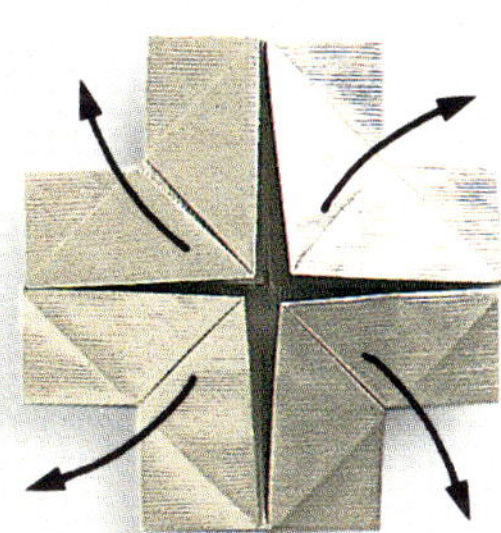

3 Fold outwards the four corners that meet at the centre.

4 Turn the shape over.

5 There is a rectangle on each side of the square. Lift one outer corner of one of the rectangles . . .

6 . . . vertically upwards . . .

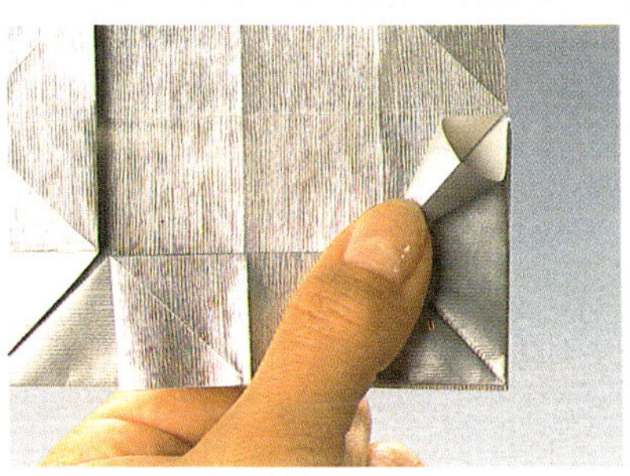

7 . . . open it out, and press it down flat.

8 Repeat with the other outer corner of this rectangle. Repeat with the other three rectangles. The picture frame is ready.
As a variation, turn back the four corners on the dotted lines.

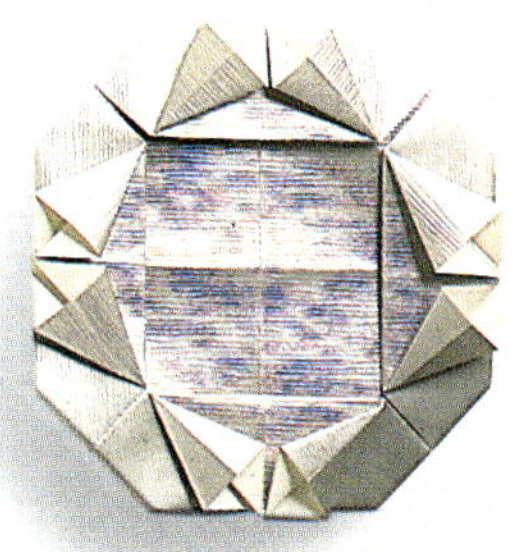

9 You can hang the frame up or, if you turn it round and half open two of the large triangles at the back, it will stand up on its own.

BASIC SHAPE V

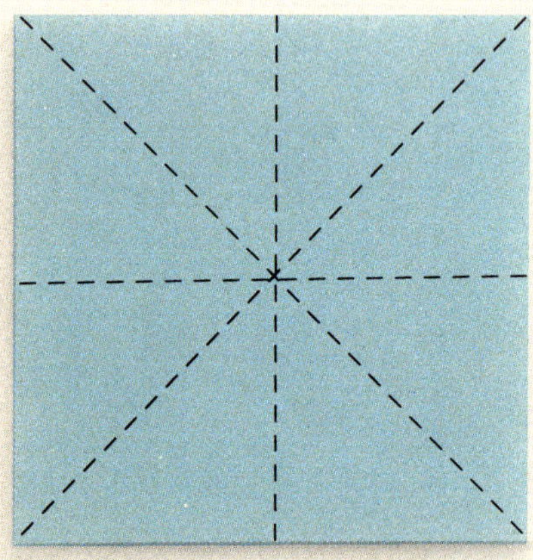

1 Fold a square piece of paper twice across the centre and twice diagonally . . .

2 . . . then unfold it again.

3 Fold the paper in half, white side inwards.

4 Lift the right half of the paper at 90° to the left half . . .

5 . . . open it out . . .

6 . . . and press it apart.

7 Fold it out flat. Lift the left wing across . . .

8 . . . to join the right one.

9 Repeat steps 3–6 with the left half of the shape.

10 This is Basic Shape V.

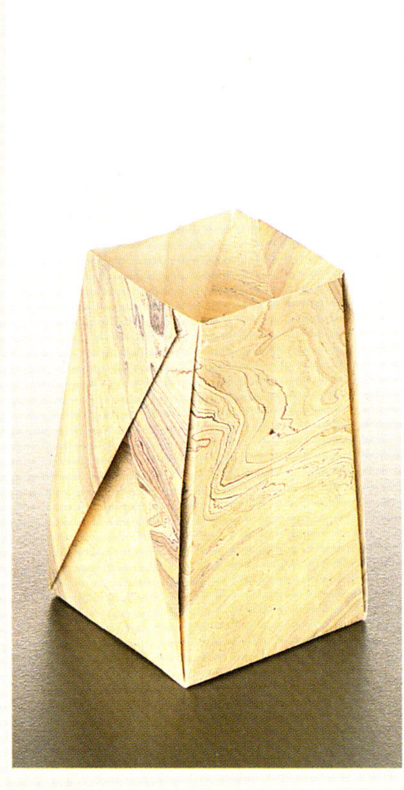

VASE

1 Begin with Basic Shape V, point downwards. Along the dotted line, fold the upper left triangle over …

2 … to the right. Fold the tip of this triangle over to the left along the dotted line.

3 Fold the protruding triangle over along the dotted line …

4 … inside the shape.

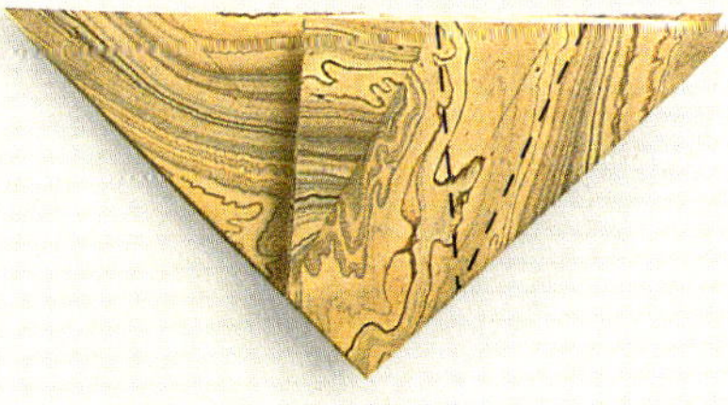

5 Fold the upper righthand triangle to the left on dotted line 1. Fold its tip back to the right on dotted line 2.

6 Repeat steps 3 and 4. Turn the shape round and repeat the whole process on the reverse side.

7 Make a sharp crease along the dotted line.

8 Open out the vase. Push the base into a square, using the crease you have just made.

9 The finished vase.

BUTTERFLY

Stick two equal sized squares of different coloured paper together and use as one sheet.

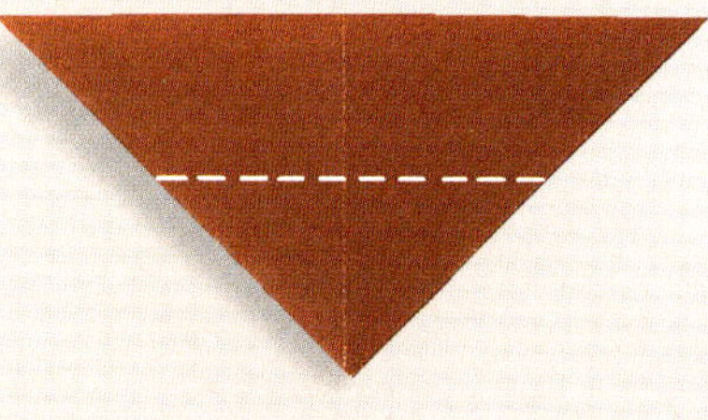

1 Start with Basic Shape V (p.34), point downwards.

2 Fold the point up along the dotted line and turn the shape over.

3 Open the shape out to reveal the inside.

4 Press the inside square shape flat. Fold the upper layers of the bottom half of the butterfly up along the dotted lines. Crease and fold back.

5 Open out the central square by lifting its bottom two corners over the creases towards the horizontal centre folds.

6 Press the new shape flat. Cut along the dotted line . . .

7 . . . to the centre. Fold the resulting triangles along the dotted lines . . .

8 . . . to the right and left.

9 Fold the shape in half.

10 Open out the wings and fold them over, making a sharp crease along the dotted line. This is the simple butterfly.

11 For the more elaborate butterfly, open up the shape again and turn it over. Along the dotted line . . .

12 . . . fold the point down. Turn the shape over.

13 Along the dotted lines . . .

14 . . . fold the two wingtips down.

15 Fold the shape in half.

16 Open it out again. Using the fold lines, plump out the body and open up the wings to put the finishing touches to the butterfly.

BALLOON

1 Begin with Basic Shape V (p.34), point upwards. Fold the front right and lefthand corners up along the dotted lines ...

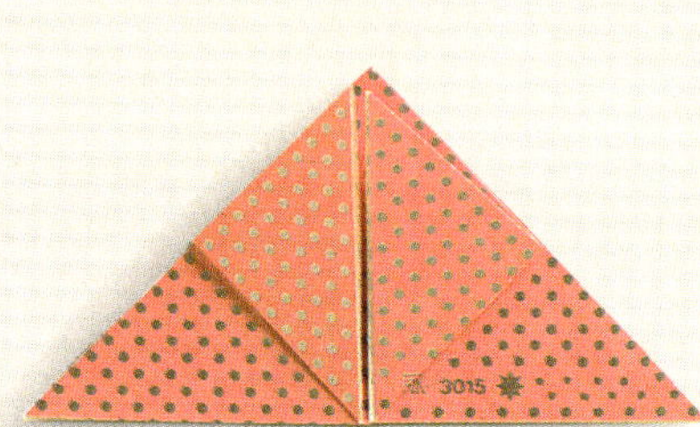

2 ... to meet at the top.

3 Turn the shape over and repeat on the reverse side. Make a crease along the horizontal. Fold the front right and lefthand triangles in along the dotted lines ...

4 ... to the centre. Repeat on the reverse side.

5 Fold the front point along the dotted line to the centre.

6 Fold the two triangles along the dotted lines, making sharp creases.

7 Fit the top triangles into the side triangles. Repeat on the reverse side.

8 Blow hard into the hole in the lower point to inflate the balloon.

AQUARIUM SCENE

BASIC SHAPE VI

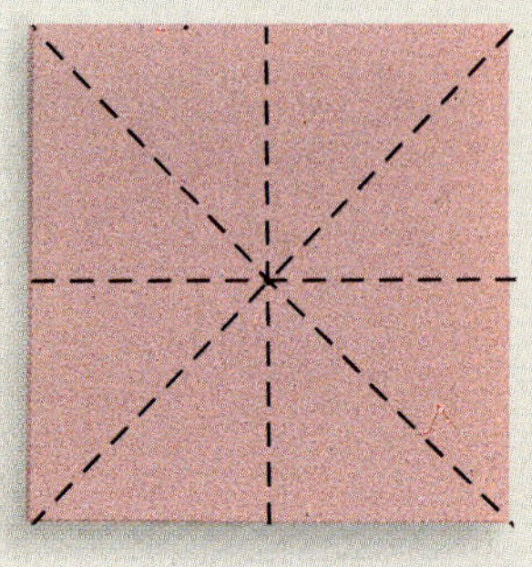

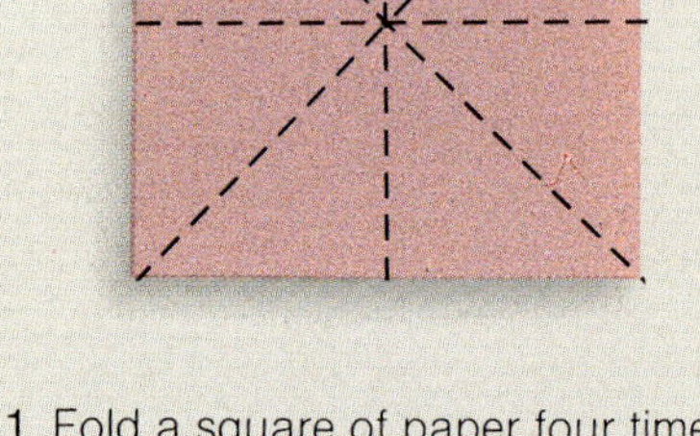

1 Fold a square of paper four times across the centre along the dotted lines, making sharp creases. Open it out.

2 Fold it over diagonally, white side inside.

3 Lift the righthand side of the paper 90° to the lefthand side . . .

4 . . . open it out and . . .

5 . . . press it down flat.

6 Make a sharp crease. Fold the left wing over . . .

7 . . . to join the right wing.

8 Repeat steps 3–7 with the left half of the shape.

9 This is Basic Shape VI.

VIOLETS

1 Start with Basic Shape VI, open point upwards. Fold the front left and righthand corners in along the dotted lines . . .

2 . . . to the middle. Repeat on the reverse side.

3 Fold the front lower triangles up along the dotted lines . . .

4 . . . so that the lower edges meet at the centre fold.

5 Repeat on the reverse side. Make a sharp crease along the dotted line.

6 Open out the front of the shape.

7 The violet is finished. Make a stem with a length of fine wire, push it up through the centre of the flower and loop it over to fix the stamens in place.

ROSE

The rose is made by combining the steps of Basic Shapes IV and VI.

1 Take a large square of paper (about 24 cm square) and fold it as shown. Unfold it.

2 Fold the four corners to the centre point, white side facing in.

3 Fold the four corners of the new square in to the centre point.

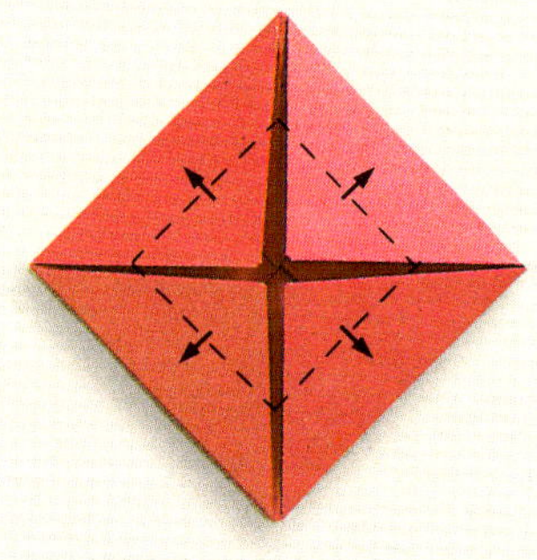

4 For the third time, fold the four corners to the centre point. Along the dotted lines . . .

5 . . . fold the four inner corners outwards so that they touch the centre of the four sides of the square. Now continue as for Basic Shape VI. Make two sharp creases along the dotted lines.

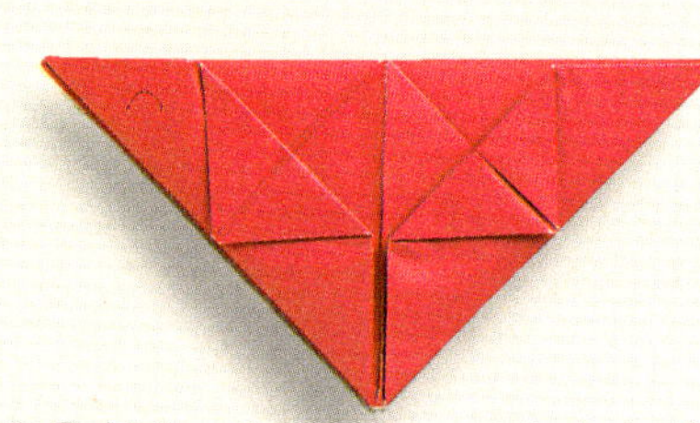

6 Fold the shape diagonally in half with the previous folds outermost.

7 Lift the righthand side of the paper at 90° to the lefthand side . . .

8 ... open it out ...

9 ... press it apart and fold it down.

10 Fold the resulting lefthand wing across ...

11 ... to join the righthand wing. Turn the shape over. Repeat the folds from step 7.

12 New version of Basic Shape VI.

13 Hold the base of the shape open in your fingers.

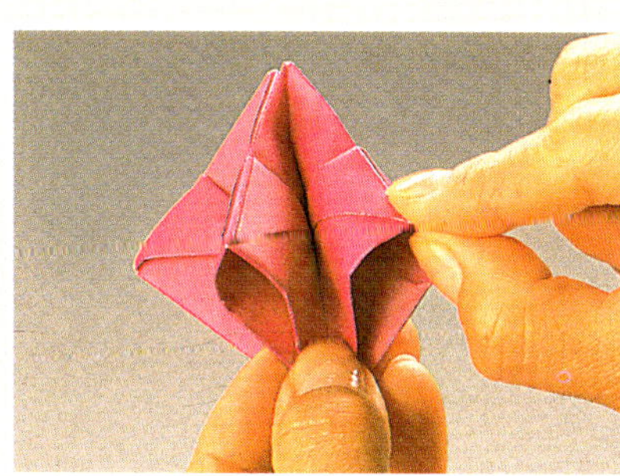

14 Open out the four points.

15 Gently open out the outer petals.

16 Open the middle petals.

17 Do the same with the inner petals.

18 The rose is finished. Fix a wire stem to the base and wrap it round with green tape.

STAR-SHAPED BOX

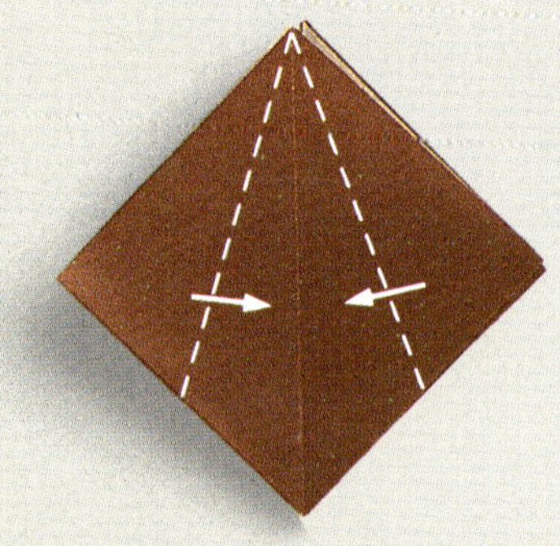

1 Start with Basic Shape VI (p.40), open point uppermost. Fold the front left and right triangles along the dotted lines . . .

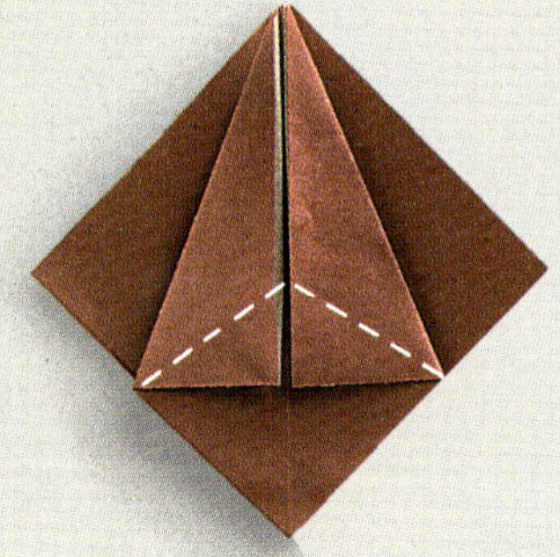

2 . . . in to the centre fold. Make two sharp creases along the dotted lines.

3 Lift one of the wings diagonally . . .

4 . . . open it out . . .

5 . . . and press it down flat.

6 Crease it into place.

7 Repeat with the other wing. Turn the shape over and repeat steps 2–6 on the reverse side. Along the dotted lines . . .

8 ... fold both outer wings in to the centre.

9 Press the shape flat, turn it over and repeat on the reverse side.

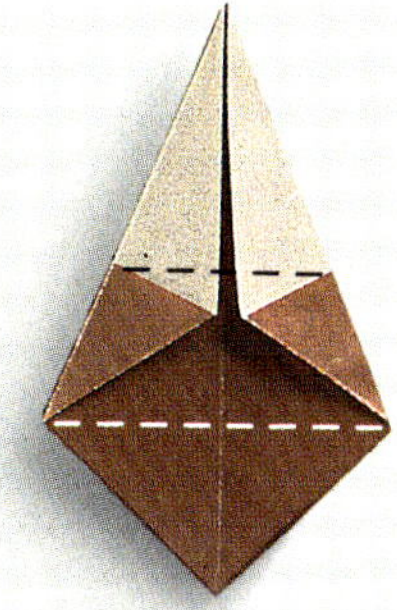

10 Make two sharp creases along the dotted lines.

11 Fold the top front point down. Fold the top back point down behind the shape. Make sharp creases to hold the folds.

12 Pull the left and righthand points carefully apart, slowly opening the star-shaped box.

13 Firm up the top edges of the box.

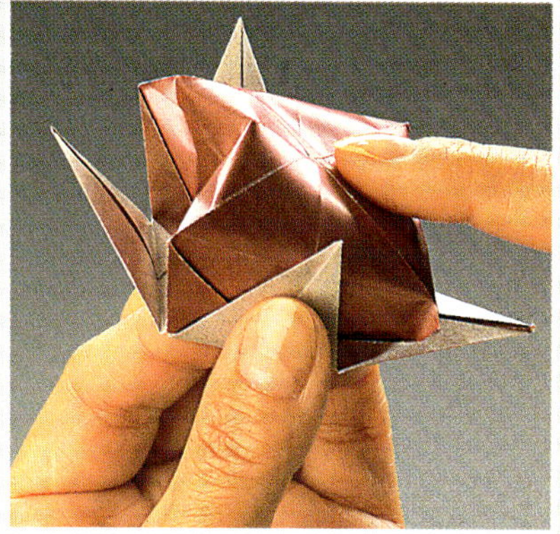

14 Using the foldlines, push out the square base of the box.

15 Firm up the base edges.

16 The finished box.

LILY

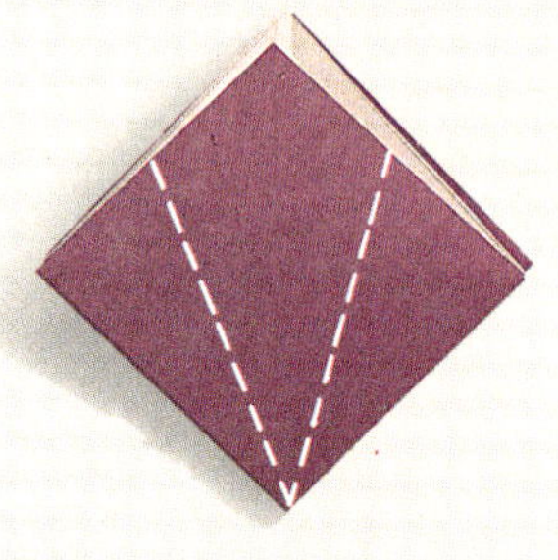

1 Begin with Basic Shape VI (p.40), open corner upwards. Make two sharp creases on the dotted lines.

2 Lift the front righthand wing up vertically ...

3 ... open it out ...

4 ... and press it apart so that the vertical folds lie on top of one another and the shape looks like a mouth.

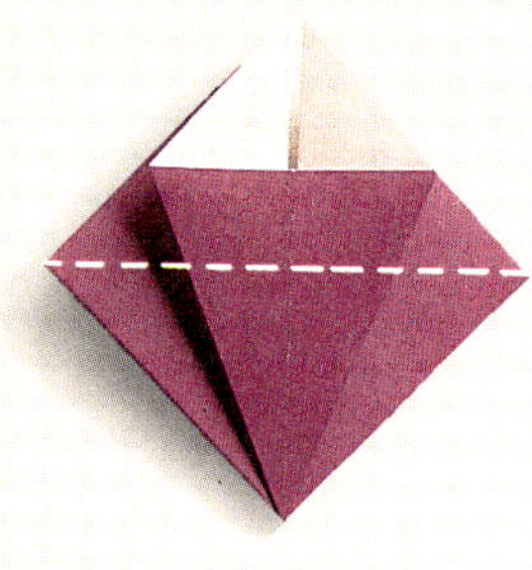

5 Press the folds in place. Make a sharp crease along the dotted line.

6 Fold the upper right and lefthand edges of the 'mouth' in to the vertical centre fold and open them again.

7 Open the 'mouth'.

8 Press the corners of the 'mouth' inwards to the centre fold, so that the edges of the paper meet on the fold.

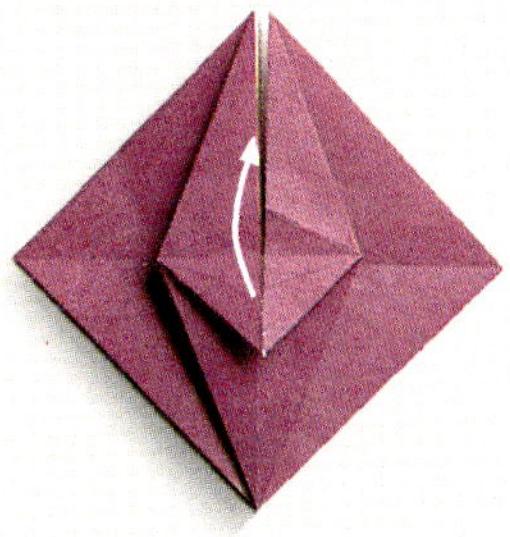

9 Press the shape flat. Fold the small triangle ...

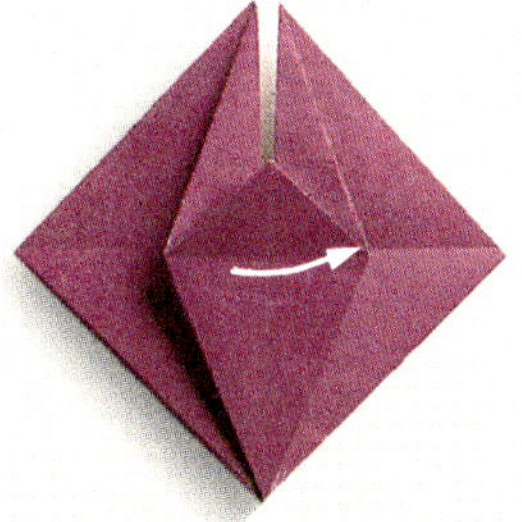

10 ... up on the horizontal centre line. Fold the left wing ...

11 ... across to meet the right.

12 Repeat steps 2–11 with the front lefthand side.

13 Turn the shape over and repeat steps 2–12 on the reverse side. All four sides are now rhomboid in shape. On a plain unfolded side, along the dotted lines ...

14 ... fold the front lower left and righthand edges in to the centre.

15 Repeat step 14 on the other three unfolded sides. Make a sharp crease on the dotted line.

16 Carefully pull apart the front and back petals.

17 Carefully pull out the left and righthand petals.

18 This is an iris.

19 Curl the outer petals round a pencil, and the iris turns into ...

20 ... a lily.

5 Repeat on the other three plain sides.

FROG

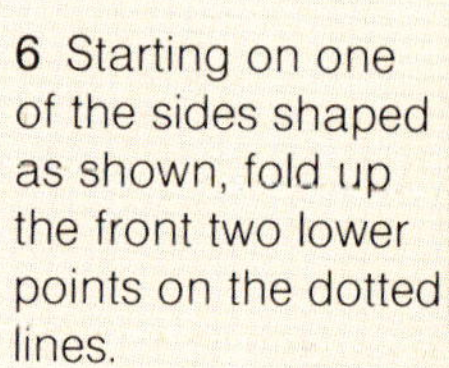

6 Starting on one of the sides shaped as shown, fold up the front two lower points on the dotted lines.

1 Follow instructions for the lily (p.46) up to step 9. Without folding the small triangle up, continue ...

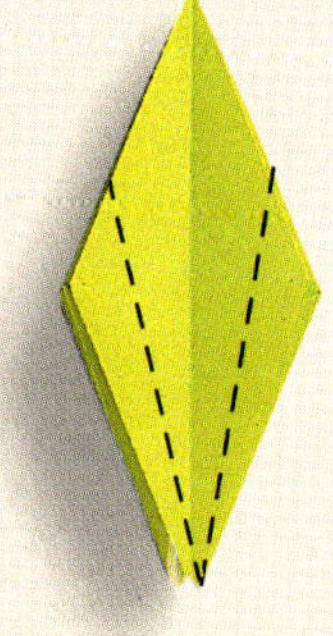

3 ... so that you end with a rhombus. Starting on a plain unfolded side, fold the front left and righthand sections in on the dotted line ...

2 ... to step 13. Repeat this process with the other three sides ...

4 ... to the middle.

7 Unfold them again.

8 Open out the left and righthand wings.

9 Fold them up as shown and make a firm crease.

10 These are the frog's front legs.

11 Shape the forelegs and hindlegs by folding along the dotted lines. First for the hindlegs . . .

12 . . . fold along the dotted lines and make a crease. Unfold.

13 Open the outside of the leg.

14 Push it inside out through the same crease. Do the same with the knee bends. Fold up the foot. Fold up the forelegs twice as shown.

15 Blow the frog's body up through the hole between its back legs. Gently push into shape.

16 The finished frog. Paint or stick on its eyes.

5 ... until the central fold is at 90° to the spine of the upright triangle.

CRAB

1 Begin with step 10 of the lily (p.47).

3 ... fold the front lefthand point out to the left. Unfold.

6 Fold the small triangle back into position. Repeat with the front right-hand point. Fold the tip of the small triangle up on the dotted line ...

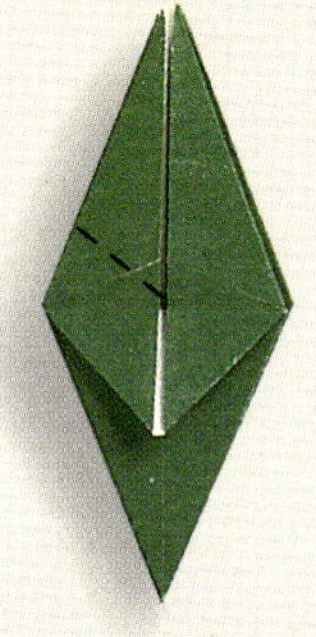

2 Repeat these folds on the other three sides. Fold the small triangle down on the centre fold. On the dotted line ...

4 Open the wing from the outside and pull the point down ...

7 ... to the centre point. Make creases on the claws and back legs along the dotted lines.

8 Open up the right claw.

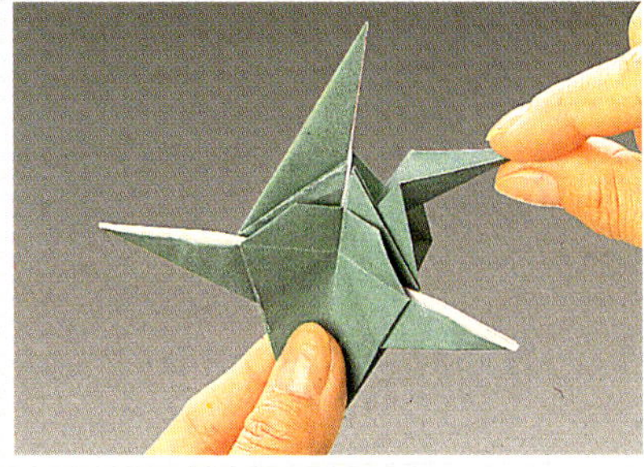

9 Turn the claw inside out along the crease line. Repeat with the other claws and the back legs.

10 Repeat steps 7–9 along the dotted lines.

11 Make sharp creases along the dotted lines.

12 Open out the two tiny top points. These are the eyes.

13 Turn the claw points over to the opposite side to round them out.

14 Turn the crab over.

15 Fold the top of the body to the inside on the dotted line. Fold the lower part of the body up on the upper line, and down on the lower line.

16 Turn the crab over again.

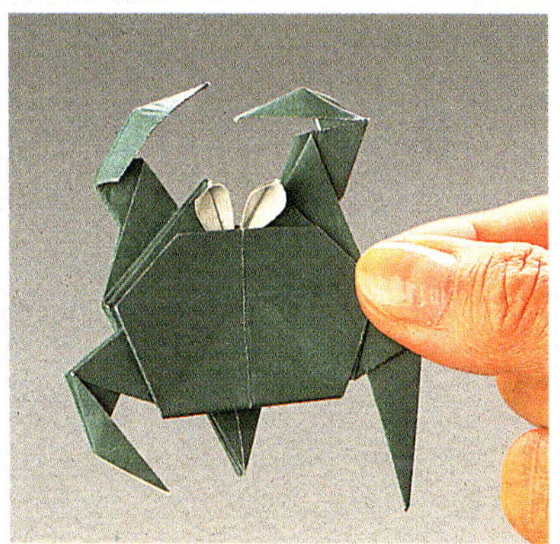

17 This is the finished crab.

WATERLILY

1 Take a sheet of thin paper about 24 cm square. Prefold the paper on the dotted lines.

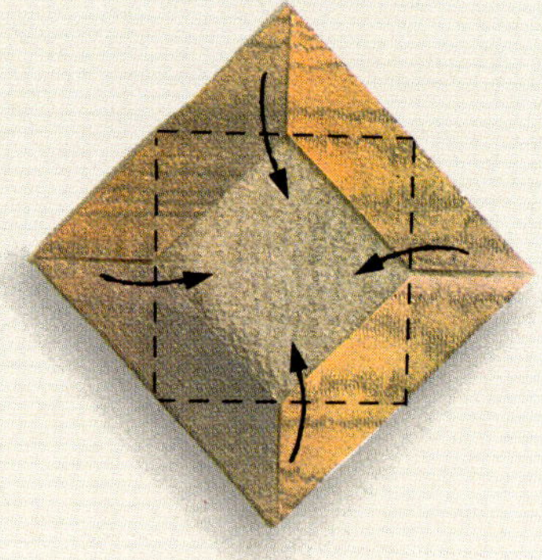

2 Fold the corners over on the first crease line to meet the second crease line. Fold the sides in again on the second crease line. Fold the four corners in ...

3 ... to meet at the middle. Make creases on the dotted lines.

4 Fold the shape diagonally in half.

5 Lift the right half of the shape up vertically.

6 Open the fold and press it apart. Fold it flat.

7 Fold the resulting lefthand triangle over ...

8 ... to join the right.

9 Repeat steps 5–8 with the left half of the shape.

10 Lift the front righthand triangle vertically.

11 Open it out and fold it flat.

12 Make a crease along the centre line.

13 Fold the top right and lefthand sections of the inner 'mouth' shape over on the dotted lines to meet at the centre. Open them again.

14 Open out the 'mouth' shape.

15 Push the left and righthand corners of the 'mouth' in to meet at the centre line.

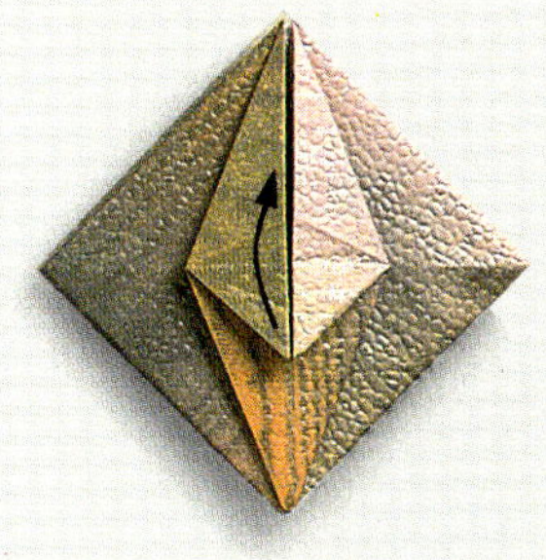

16 Fold the resulting small triangle up on the centre line . . .

17 . . . and the left wing over to meet the right.

18 Repeat steps 9–17 with the other three sides.

19 Fold the front and back triangles out from the shape.

20 Pull the right and lefthand points downwards.

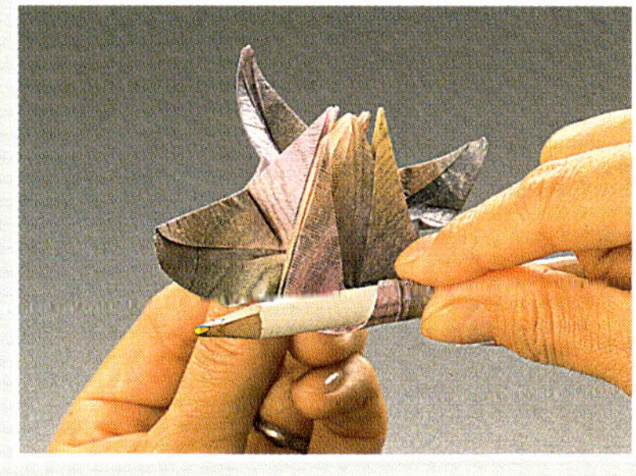

21 Turn the shape upside down so that the open points are uppermost. Curl the petals round a pencil.

22 Open the inner petals and curl them over.

BASIC SHAPE VII

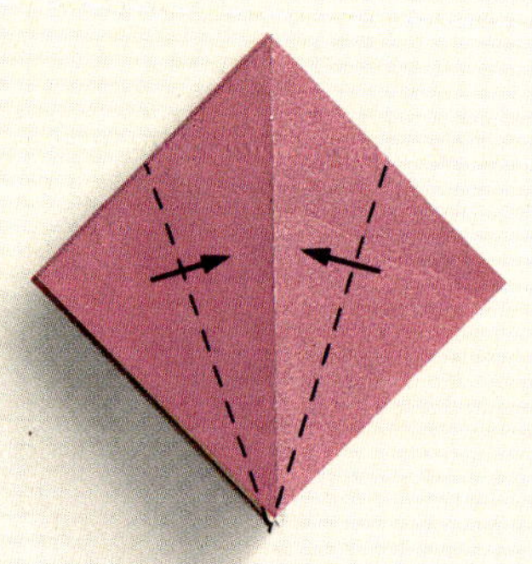

1 Begin with Basic Shape VI (p.40), open point downwards. Along the dotted lines ...

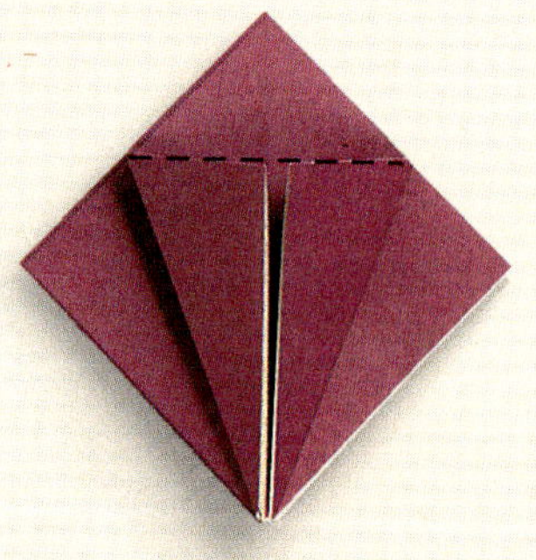

2 ... fold the front left and righthand sections in to meet at the centre fold. Along the dotted line ...

3 ... fold the corner down.

4 Unfold the last three folds.

5 Gently lift the lower front point.

6 Fold the point up to the top on the crease you have already made.

7 Flatten the left and righthand corners of the 'mouth' shape so that the sides meet in the middle.

8 Make the creases sharp and turn the shape over. Repeat the folds on the reverse side.

9 This is Basic Shape VII.

FLYING CRANE

5 Fold the lefthand point inside out on the crease you have just made. This is the head.

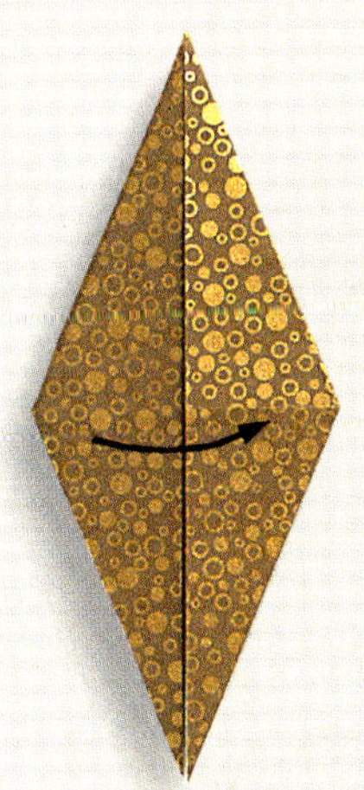

1 Begin with Basic Shape VII (p.54), open point downwards.

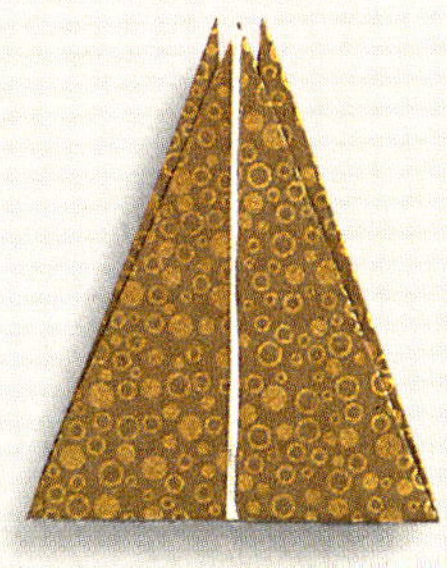

3 . . . fold the bottom point up. Repeat on the reverse side.

6 Roll the wings around a pencil to give them shape.

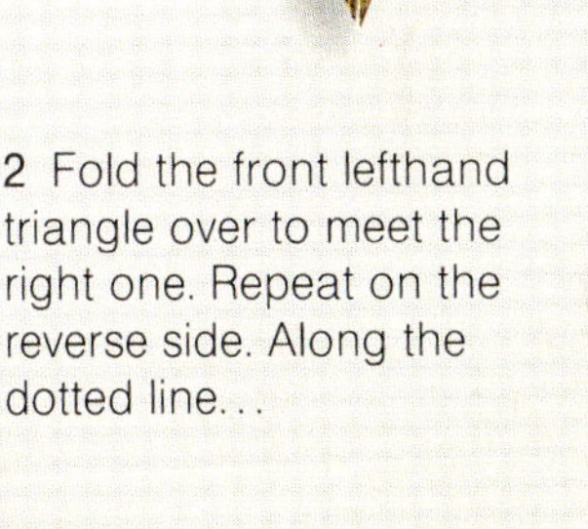

2 Fold the front lefthand triangle over to meet the right one. Repeat on the reverse side. Along the dotted line. . .

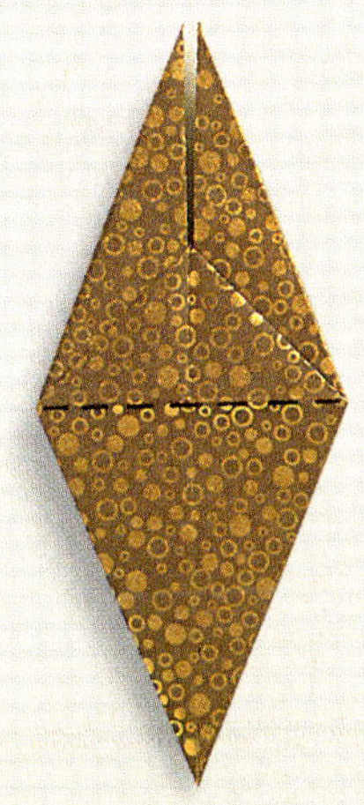

4 Pull the right and lefthand points out to the sides. Fold to hold them in place. Make a crease along the horizontal white line.

7 Hold the crane's breast and gently move its tail to make it flap its wings.

STARS

STAR A

1 Begin with Basic Shape VII (p.54), open point upwards.

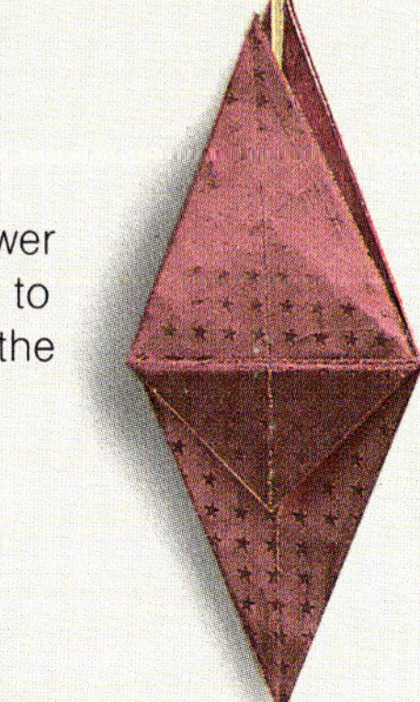

2 Fold the lower front point up to the top. Turn the shape over.

3 Along the dotted lines, fold the top two points ...

4 ... down to the sides and back up again.

5 Lift the lefthand wing to the vertical ...

6 ... open it out and press it apart. Fold it flat.

7 Repeat with the righthand wing.

8 Stick three stars on top of one another to make star A.

STAR B

1 Start the Basic Shape VII (p.54), open point downwards.

2 Open out both wings on the lefthand side.

3 Fold the lefthand point up through the centre on the top. Close the lefthand side.

4 Repeat with the righthand side. Along the dotted lines . . .

5 . . . fold the lower front edges up to the centre line. Repeat on the back.

6 Pick up the shape, holding the back and front wings together at the corners.

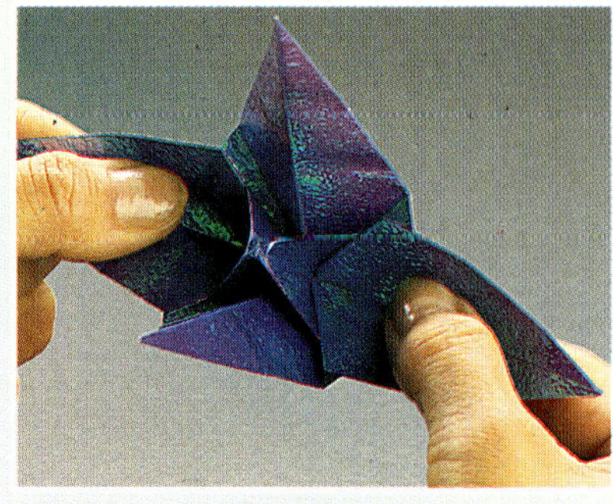

7 Pull the wings gently apart . . .

8 . . . until a square appears in the middle.

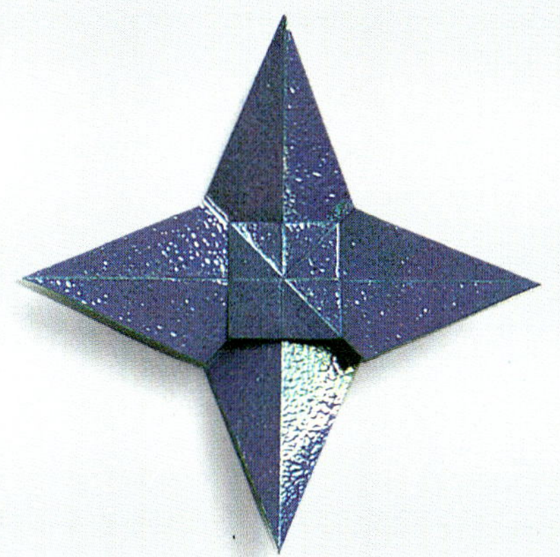

9 Press the shape flat and turn it over.

10 Take one of the four small central triangles ...

11 ... and lift it vertically.

12 Open it out and press it apart.

13 Repeat with the other three triangles. Along the dotted lines ...

14 ... fold the short edges in to meet at the centre. Make a crease along the dotted lines.

15 Open the folds. Pull the point up gently.

16 Push the corners in to the centre. Repeat all round the star. Turn it over.

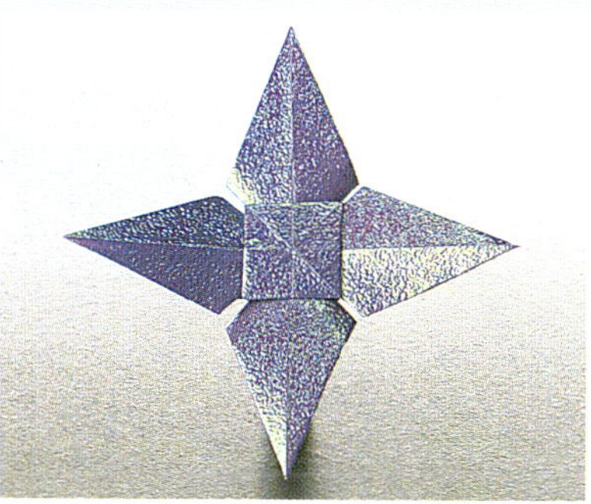

17 This is star B.

RABBIT

1 Begin with step 7 of Basic Shape VII (p.54). Turn the shape over.

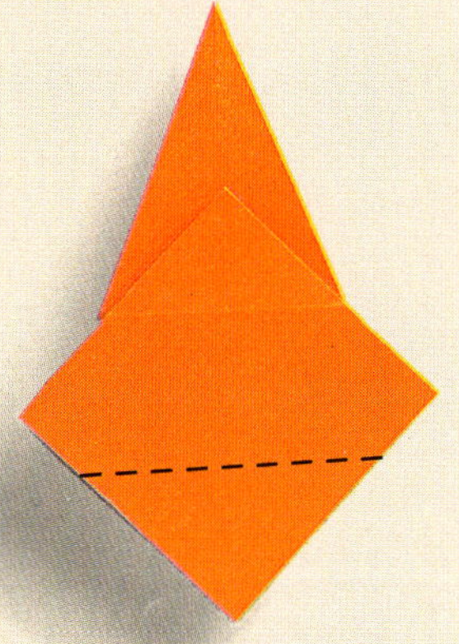

2 Along the dotted line ...

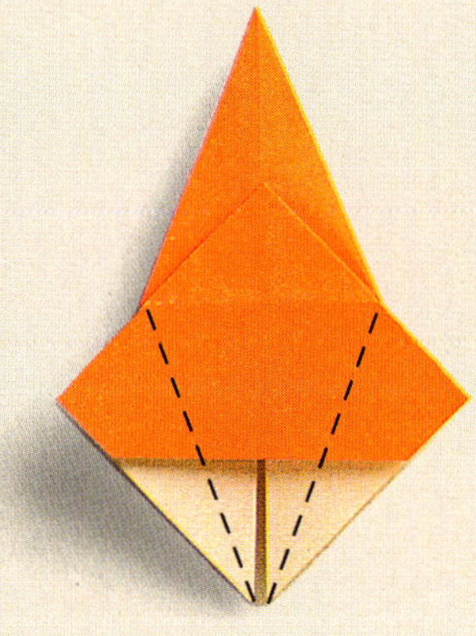

3 ... fold the lower front triangle to the inside. Along the dotted lines ...

4 ... fold the lower left and righthand sections inwards. Turn the shape over.

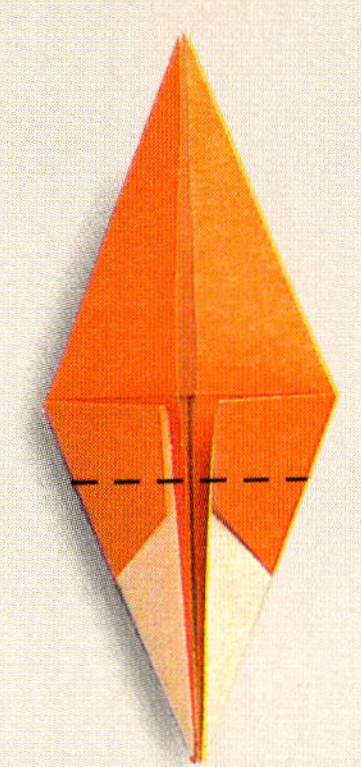

5 Along the dotted line ...

6 ... fold the shape up.

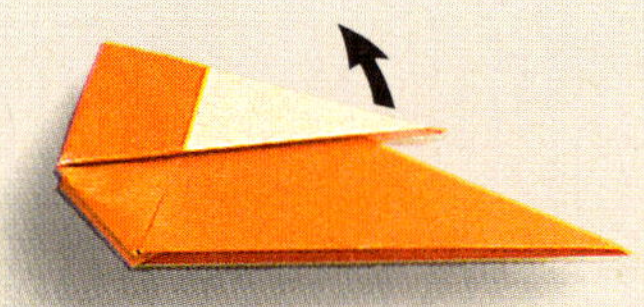

7 Fold the shape in half so that both points are on the outside. Turn the shape so that they point to the right. Lift both points gently upwards ...

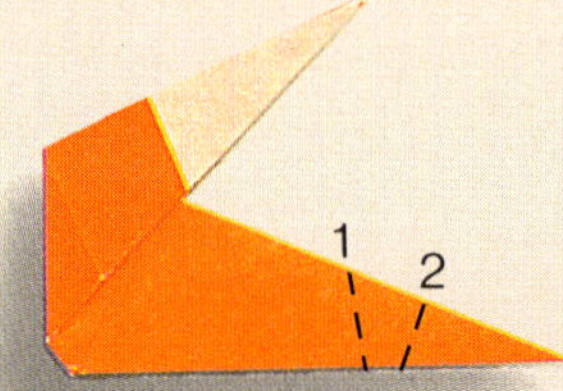

8 ... and press the shape flat. Make sharp creases on the dotted lines.

9 Fold the point inwards on the first crease . . .

10 . . . and outwards on the second crease.

11 Make a crease on the dotted line.

12 Fold the tail down through the crease you have just made.

13 Fold each ear downwards on the dotted line.

14 Make a crease on the dotted line. Repeat on the other side.

15 Turn in the corners on the creases you have just made.

16 Open out the ears . . .

17 . . . and fold them forwards.

18 Make a sharp crease on each ear on the dotted line.

19 Open out the ears again, and the rabbit is ready.

DEVIL MASK

1 Begin with Basic Shape VII (p.54), the open point to the left. Take both the lefthand points . . .

2 . . . and open them out until . . .

3 . . . the paper is quite flat.

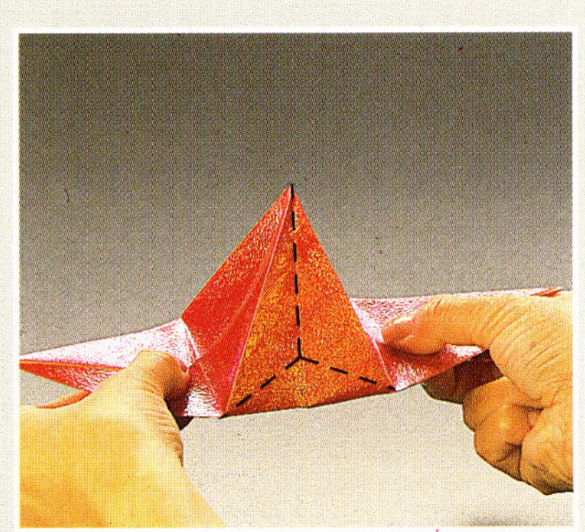

4 Turn it over. Along the dotted lines . . .

5 . . . press both upright points together in the middle and . . .

6 . . . run your thumbnails down the creases to the base.

7 Fold the paper in the middle.

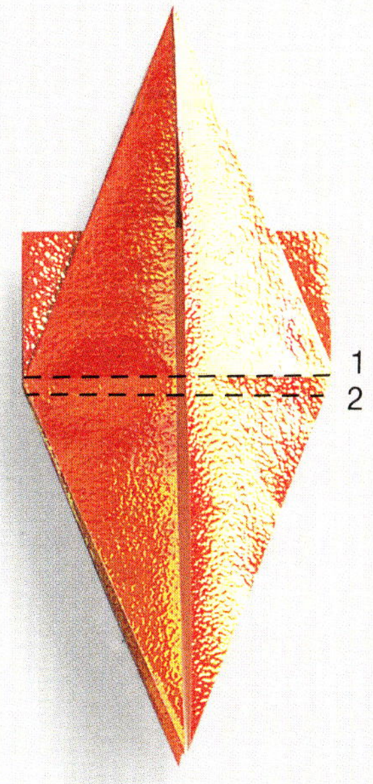

8 Make two parallel creases along the dotted lines. Fold the lower front triangle up to the inside on crease 1 and . . .

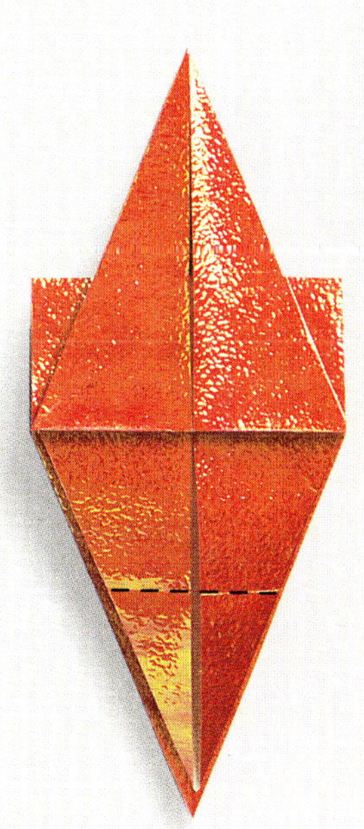

9 . . . down to the outside on crease 2. Along the dotted line, fold the lower front triangle up.

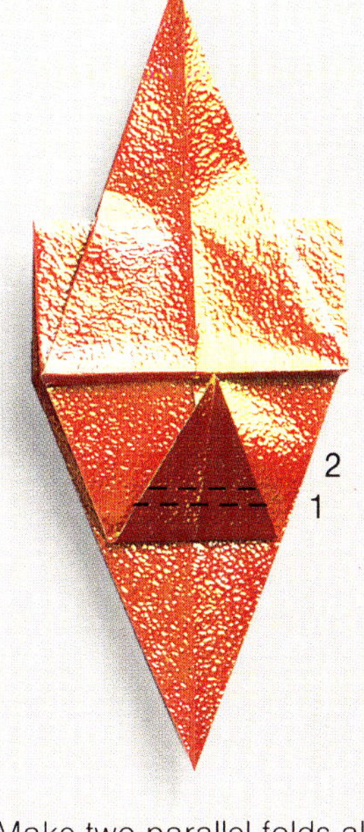

10 Make two parallel folds along the dotted lines.

11 Fold the triangle down on line 1 and up on line 2 to make the nose. Fold the lower triangle up on line 1 and down on line 2 to make the mouth. For the eyebrows fold the paper up along dotted lines 3 and 4. Fold the corners of the eyebrows down along these dotted lines.

12 For the horns, fold the two points downwards along the dotted lines . . .

14 Fold the horns back up again, open them out . . .

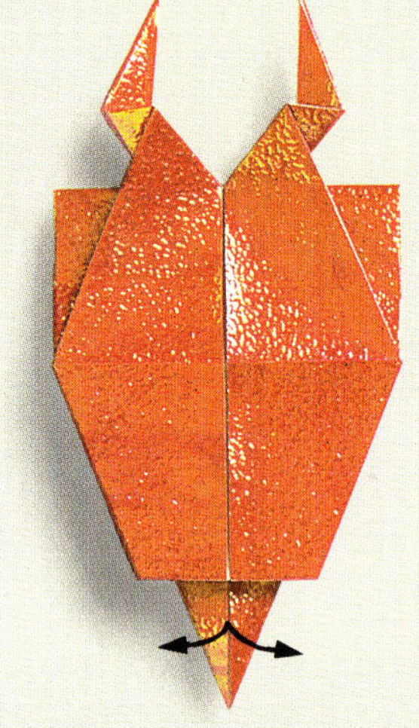

17 Open the beard out a bit . . .

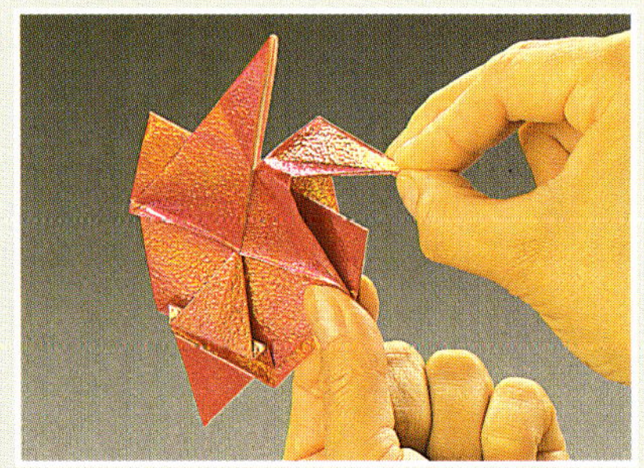

15 . . .and turn them in on the crease you have just made.

13 . . . to the right and left.

16 Repeat steps 13–15 on the points of the horns at the dotted lines. Turn the mask over.

18 . . . and press it flat.

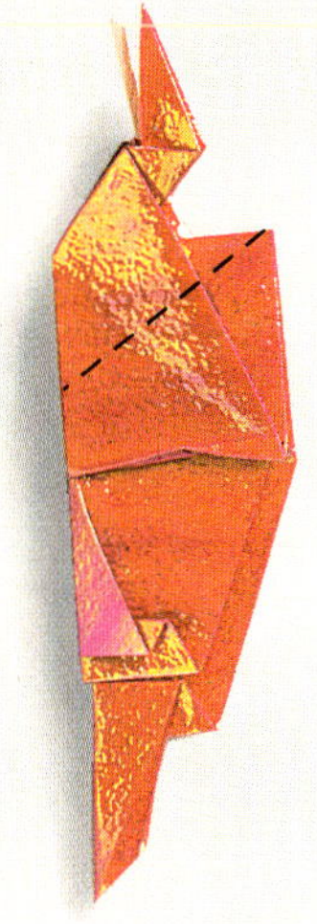

19 Fold the mask in half. Along the dotted line . . .

21 Turn the upper part of the face to the inside along the crease you have just made. Open it out.

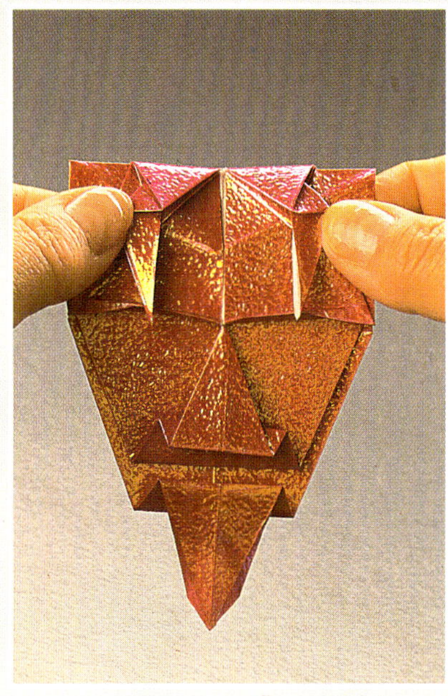

23 . . . fold the horns forwards. Release them.

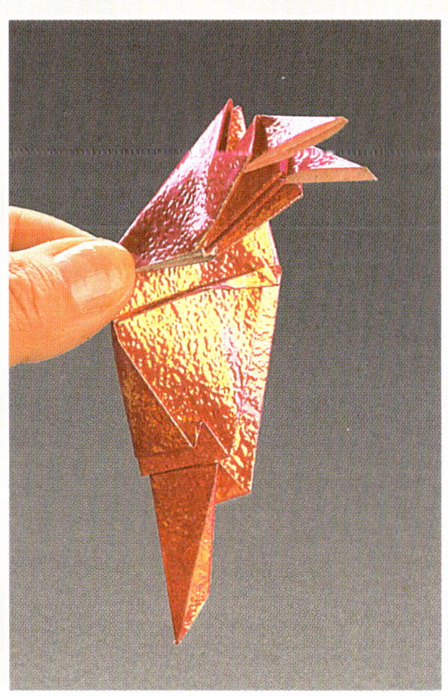

20 . . . make a crease.

22 Along the dotted lines . . .

24 Shape the nose, and the mask is finished.

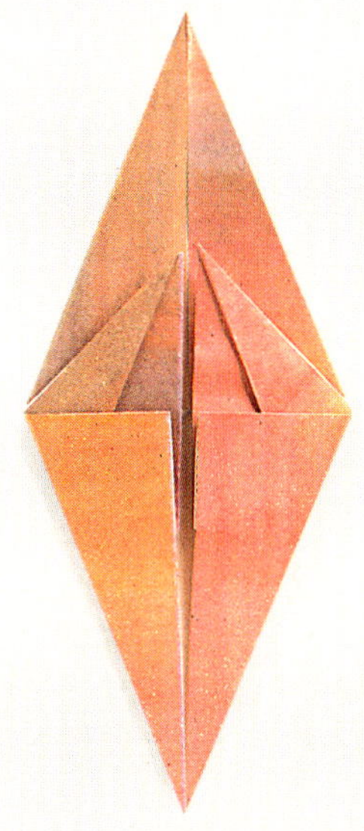

3 . . . fold the lower edges in to the centre fold.

FOX MASK

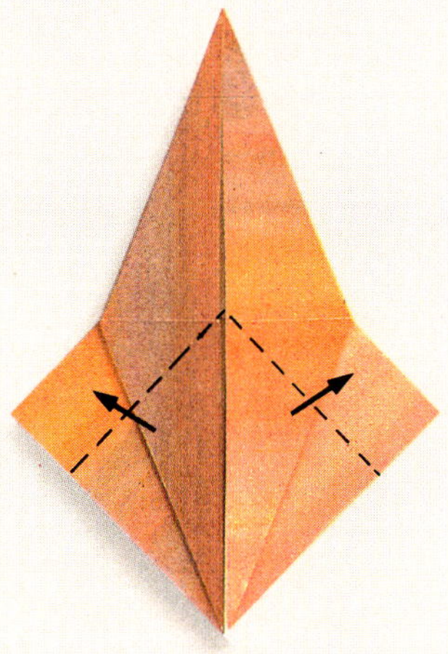

1 Begin with step 7 of Basic Shape VII (p.54). Along the dotted lines . . .

2 . . . fold the two lower front wings up to the horizontal. Along the dotted lines . . .

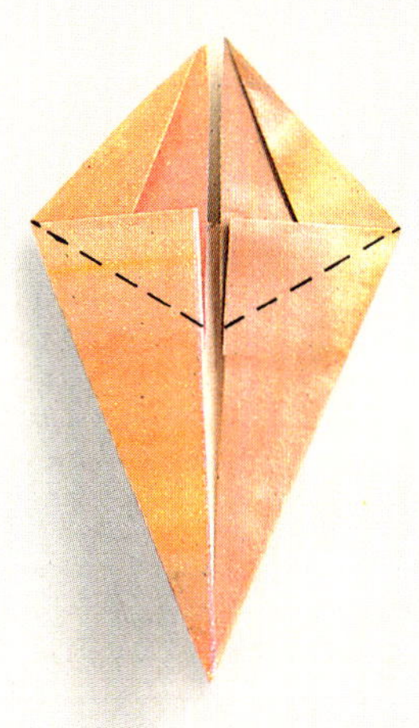

4 Fold the top point back on the horizontal centre fold. Along the dotted lines . . .

5 ... fold the two centre corners down.

8 Fold the corners of the resulting shapes in on the dotted lines to the centre.

11 ... and press the corners in to the centre. Press them flat.

6 Fold them back up again, stand them vertical ...

9 Make thumbnail creases along the dotted lines.

12 Along the dotted line ...

7 ... open them out and press them flat.

10 Open out the folds ...

13 ... fold the lower front point up. Along the dotted lines ...

14 ... fold both points over to the left.

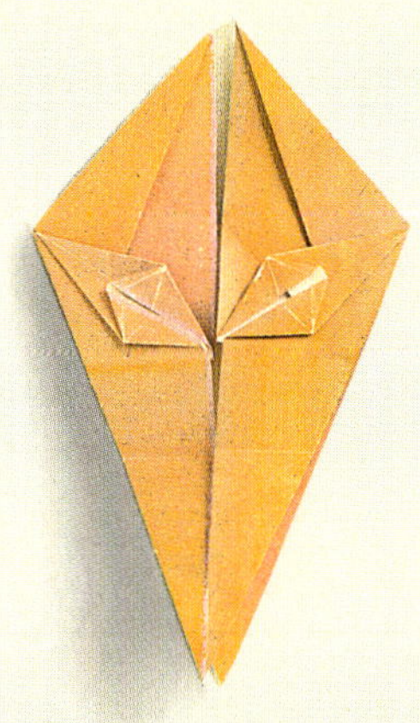

15 Unfold them again. Fold the front point up as in step 13 and fold both points over to the right ...

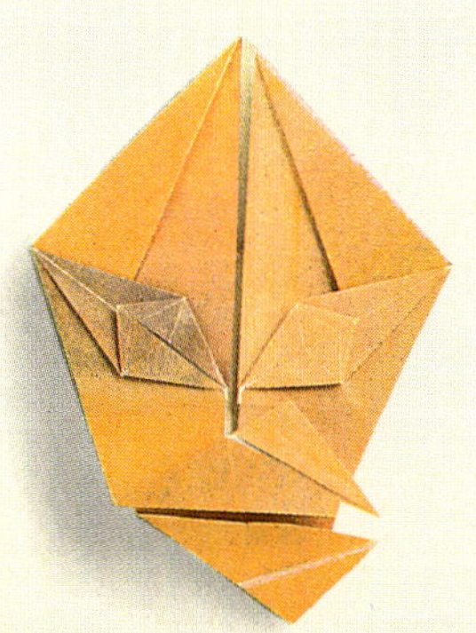

16 ... on the crease lines you have just made.

17 Open out the folds again, and fold the point up as before.

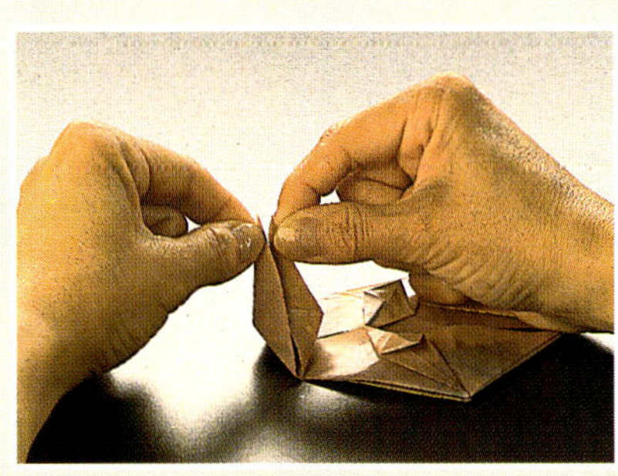

18 Lift the points up, press them together in the middle and ...

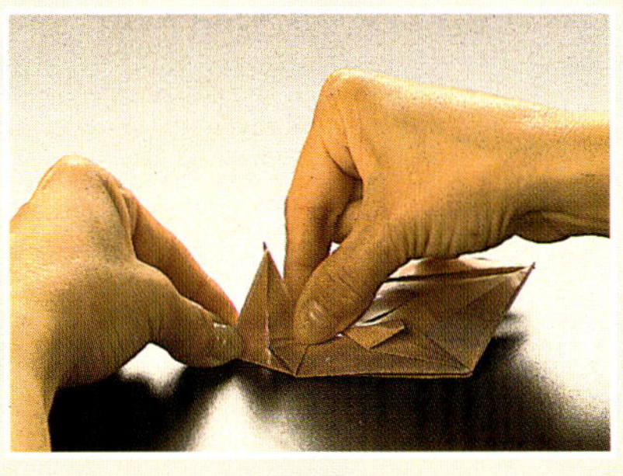

19 ... make firm creases down to the base.

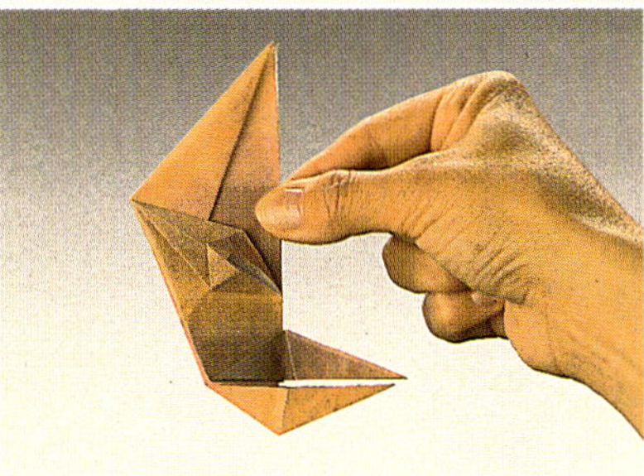

20 Fold the shape in half with the points protruding.

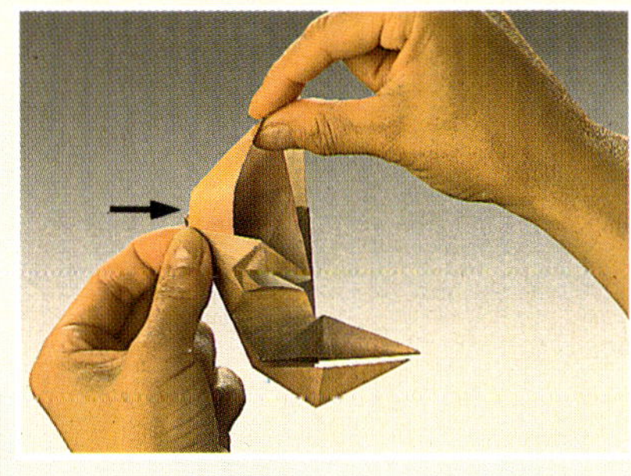

21 Open out the ears and press down at the back to keep them open.

22 The fox mask is finished.

DESERT SCENE

3 . . . fold the lower righthand triangle up. Unfold it.

CAMEL

4 Separate the righthand wings . . .

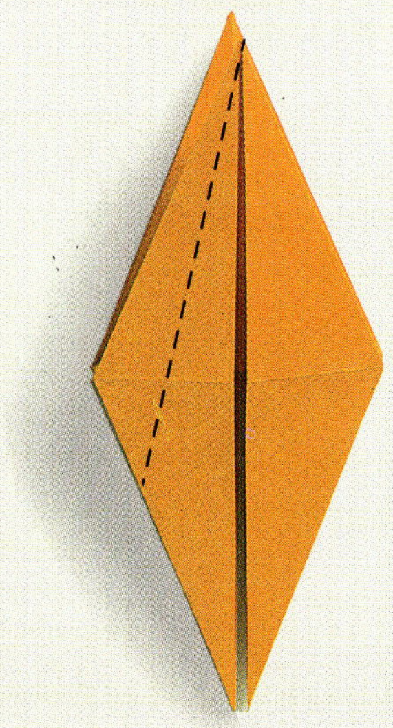

1 Begin with Basic Shape VII (p.54), open point downwards. Along the dotted line . . .

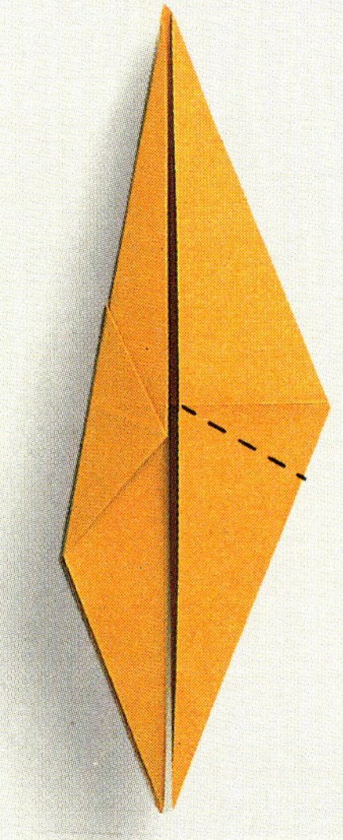

2 . . . fold the front left wing forwards and the back left wing backwards to the centre. Along the dotted line . . .

5 . . . and push the point up on the crease you have just made.

6 On dotted line 1, fold the front outer section back to the left. Make a sharp crease on dotted line 2.

7 Open the lefthand wing ...

8 ... and fold the point up on the crease you have just made.

9 Along the dotted line ...

10 ... fold the top points to the front and back.

11 Open the folds of the righthand point again. Fold the middle wing along the dotted line ...

12 ... to the right and press down the resulting triangle.

13 Repeat on the reverse side. These are the camel's front legs.

14 Make a sharp fold along the dotted line.

15 Lift up the front leg and push the corner in behind it. Repeat on the reverse side.

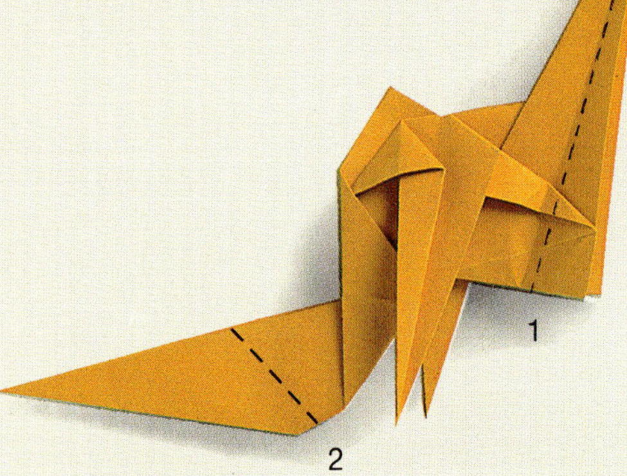

16 Fold the front of the righthand wing forwards and the back . . .

17 . . . backwards at dotted line 1. At dotted line 2, fold the lefthand wing up . . .

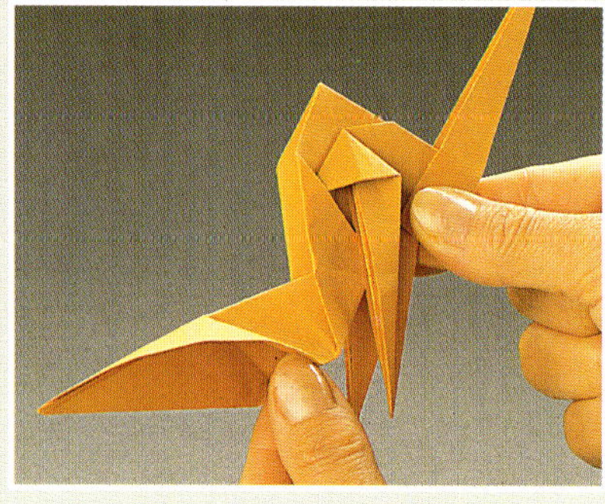

18 . . . unfold it and open out the point.

19 Fold the point back over the crease you have just made.

20 Fold the top left point over, making a sharp crease on the dotted line. Fold it back.

21 Open out the point and fold the top over . . .

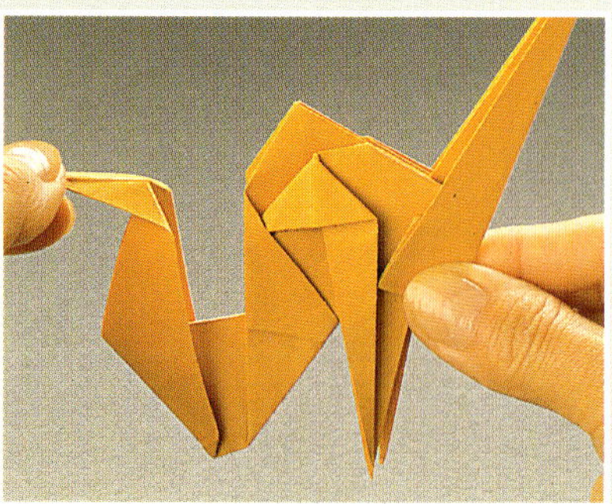

22 . . . to the left on the crease you have just made.

23 Press the neck in towards the body a little. Fold the righthand point over on the dotted line.

24 Fold it back and open out the wing.

25 Fold it down inwards through the same crease.

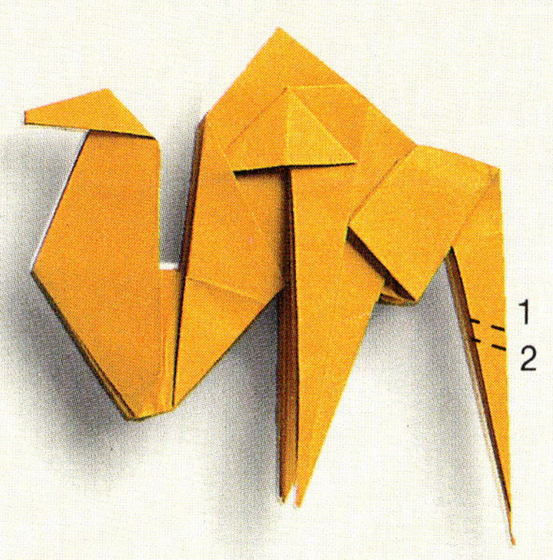

26 Make two parallel creases on the dotted lines.

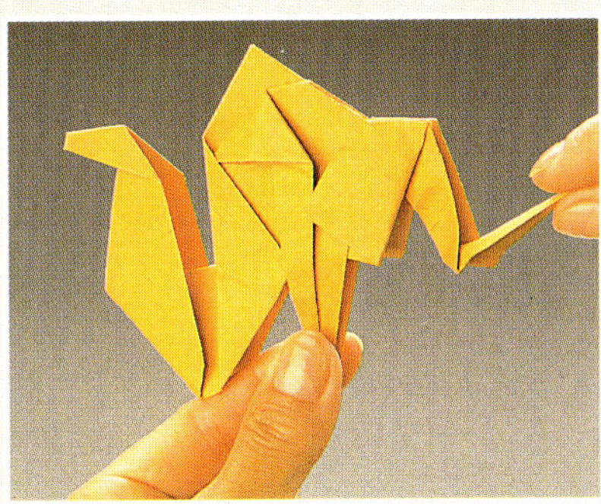

27 Open out the wing. Push the point up through the first crease . . .

28 . . . and fold it down through the second to make the back legs.

29 The camel is finished.

30 If you want to make the camel sit down, fold the forelegs to the right and the back legs to the left.

31 The sitting camel looks like this.

TALKING FISH

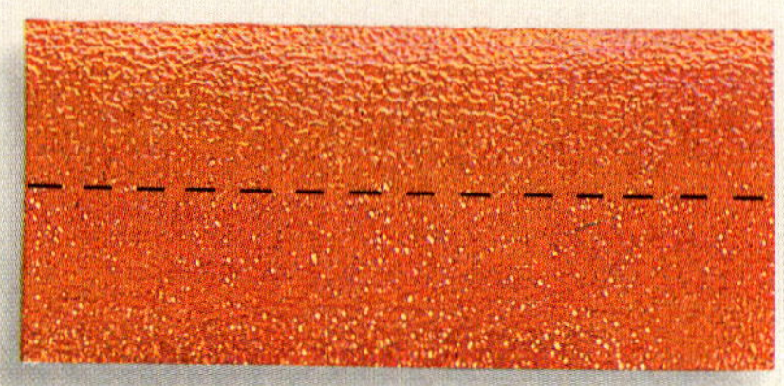

1 Take a rectangular sheet of paper. The width must be less than half the length. Fold it along the dotted line.

2 Lay the paper coloured side down. Fold all four corners in on the dotted lines . . .

3 . . . to the centre.

4 Turn the shape over. Fold the points on the dotted lines . . .

5 . . . in towards the centre.

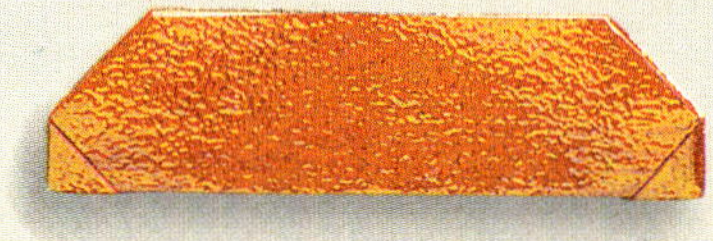

6 Fold the shape in half with the white side of the paper inside.

7 Hold the shape at either end and carefully put the right end-folds over the left end-folds.

8 Hold the mouth of the fish and push the centre crease in from the back.

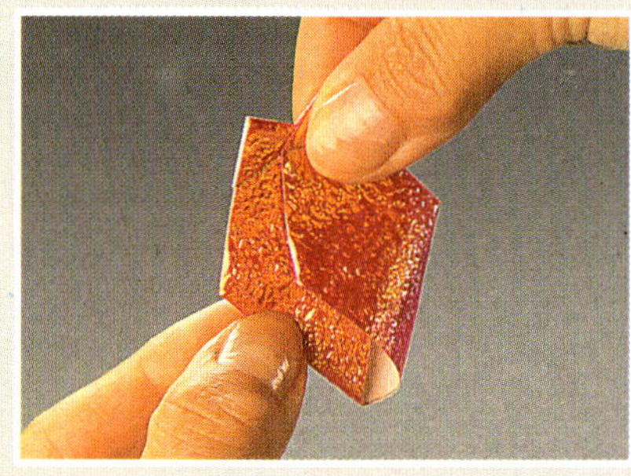

9 Align the two lower edges of the shape and press it flat.

10 Paint or stick on the eyes. Fold the tail over a little bit at both sides. The fish will speak when you pull gently on both sides of its tail.

MONKEY

1 Make a triangular sheet of paper by cutting a square sheet diagonally in half. Make creases on the dotted lines.

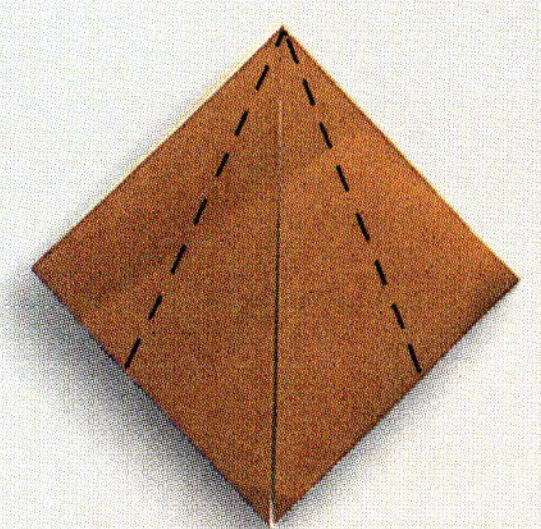

2 Fold the lower triangles up to meet at the centre. Along the dotted lines . . .

3 . . . fold the outer triangles in to meet at the centre. Unfold.

4 Open the left half of the shape . . .

5 . . . and fold the outer part of the left half in on the crease you have already made.

6 Fold the left half of the paper together again.

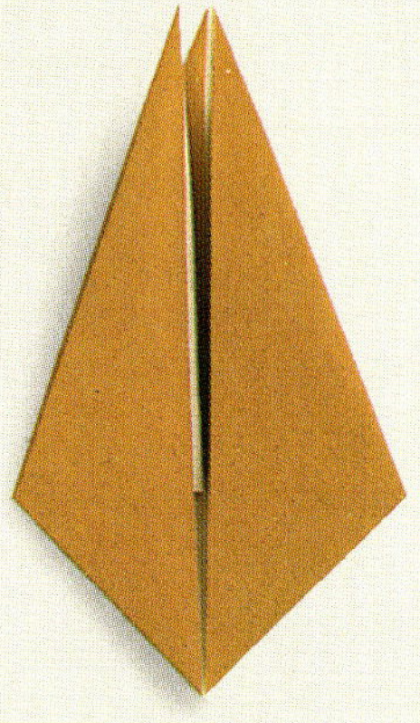

7 Repeat steps 4–6 with the right half of the shape.

8 Fold the shape in half with the unfolded side of the paper inside. Turn it over. Along the dotted line, fold the front wing to the right . . .

9 . . . and the back wing to the left. These are the arms. Fold the arms in half by folding the top part down at the centre. Turn the shape over . . .

10 . . . and fold the top point over to the right.

11 Open the point and fold it down flat to the left. This is the head.

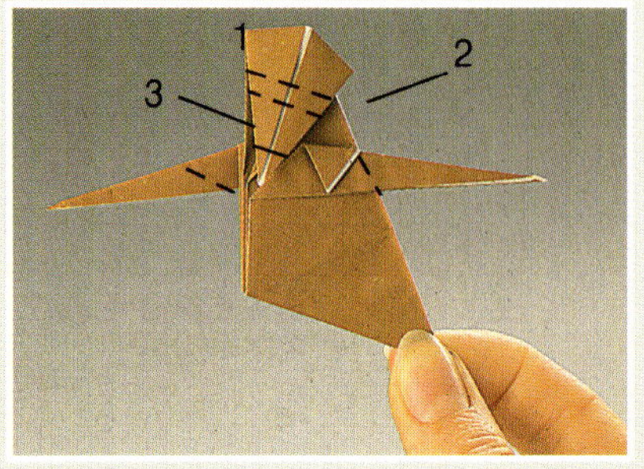

12 Make creases along the dotted lines.

13 Fold the monkey's right arm up. Fold the head in on the first crease, out on the second and in again on the third.

14 Open out the monkey's left arm from beneath.

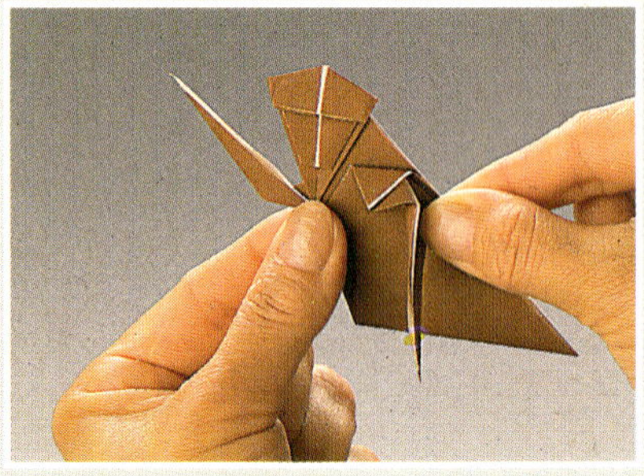

15 Fold the lower part of the arm in on the crease you have already made.